INTRO

XRP Unleashed: Exploring the Cryptocurrency and its Use Cases

Disclaimer:

INTRO

In the pulsating, rapidly-evolving realm of blockchain and cryptocurrencies, there's one name that stands out, not merely as an asset but as a revolutionary force set to transform the landscape of global finance: Ripple and its native digital currency, XRP.

Ripple, a creation of the technology company Ripple Labs Inc, is a dual entity. It's both a digital payment protocol and a cryptocurrency. The Ripple platform is an open-source blockchain-based system specifically designed to break down the barriers in international transactions. Traditional cross-border money transfers can often be a laborious process involving multiple intermediaries, a good deal of time, and substantial fees. Ripple reimagines this process, providing a seamless, swift, and cost-effective alternative.

Think of RippleNet, Ripple's payment ecosystem, as a cosmopolitan digital highway, linking together disparate financial systems, facilitating the rapid flow of money across borders. Within this ecosystem resides XRP, Ripple's native cryptocurrency, the supercharged engine that powers transactions on this highway. Unlike Bitcoin, XRP isn't created through mining. It was pre-mined and periodically released into the market by Ripple Labs, ensuring a level of stability and predictability.

But what really sets XRP apart from its peers is its astonishing speed. Picture this: a Bitcoin transaction can take hours to confirm. In contrast, an XRP transaction is lightning fast, confirmed in a mere three to five seconds. It's like comparing a horse-drawn carriage to a bullet train. Ripple doesn't just outpace Bitcoin in terms of speed. It also vastly outstrips it in terms of processing capacity. Bitcoin can manage a modest seven transactions per second, whereas Ripple handles a whopping 1,500.

Now let's venture into the realm of the possible, the future that Ripple and XRP promise. It's a world where sending money across the globe is as quick and straightforward as sending an email. Imagine a small business owner in Argentina paying a supplier in Japan instantly. Or a college student in the US receiving funds from her family in India within seconds. That's the transformative potential Ripple and XRP hold.

Ripple isn't just about transactions, though. It's also a platform for creating decentralized applications (dApps), which opens up exciting avenues. From smart contracts that automatically execute when certain conditions are met, to democratizing finance by enabling anyone to create their own tokens, the future with Ripple and XRP is a promise of endless possibilities. In this future, finance is not just faster and cheaper but also more democratic and accessible to all. Welcome to the exciting world of Ripple and XRP!

Ripple and XRP's potential doesn't stop at remittances and international payments. They are laying the foundation for a new era of decentralized finance (DeFi) — an emerging trend in finance that seeks to democratize access to financial services.

Ripple could play a crucial role in expanding the accessibility of financial products and services. It opens the gates to the financial world, allowing everyone, regardless of their location or economic status, to have equal access to a broad array of financial services. This means that an entrepreneur in a remote part of the world with limited access to traditional banking structures could secure a loan, start a business, and achieve economic mobility.

Ripple's potential for facilitating interoperability between different financial systems and cryptocurrencies could lead to a truly interconnected global economy. For instance, a user could easily convert their Bitcoin to XRP, transfer it across the globe in seconds, and then convert it into a local fiat currency — all within the Ripple ecosystem. This sort of seamless integration across different systems is one of the aspects that make Ripple a game-changer in the cryptocurrency space.

Ripple and XRP also present exciting possibilities for corporations and institutions. With Ripple's technology, banks can settle cross-border payments in real-time with end-to-end transparency and lower costs. This is an attractive proposition for financial institutions that are looking to modernize their infrastructure and offer better services to their customers.

One of the more fascinating potentials of XRP is its role as a liquidity tool. Instead of banks needing to hold various currencies in accounts around the world (known as nostro and vostro accounts), they could simply hold XRP. They could then use XRP for on-demand liquidity, transferring the exact amount necessary, reducing costs, and freeing up capital.

let's not forget Ripple's potential as a platform for building decentralized applications (dApps). Developers around the world could leverage Ripple's infrastructure to create a plethora of blockchain-based applications, from gaming to supply chain solutions, that could redefine industries.

So, get ready for the future, where the boundaries of finance blur, where transactions are as easy as a click of a button, and where financial empowerment is not a privilege, but a right.

Diving deeper into the extraordinary potential of Ripple and XRP, we uncover a treasure trove of transformative prospects. This technology brings forth an innovative wave that has the capacity to reshape industries beyond just finance.

Consider, for example, the real estate sector, an industry still largely bound by traditional, time-consuming transaction methods. Ripple's technology can simplify the property-buying process by enabling swift, secure, and cost-efficient transactions, thereby transforming the entire property landscape. A homeowner in Australia could sell their property to a buyer in the United States, and the transaction could be completed almost instantly, eliminating the need for extensive paperwork and long waiting times.

In the retail sector, Ripple and XRP can revolutionize payments by making them faster, cheaper, and more efficient. A shopper could make payments in XRP, bypassing credit card fees or bank transfer delays. In the blink of an eye, the transaction would be complete, providing a seamless retail experience for both consumers and merchants.

Ripple's infrastructure could spur a new era of decentralized finance applications, also known as DeFi. Developers could build upon Ripple's robust and fast platform to create apps offering services such as lending, borrowing, and earning interest on cryptocurrencies. This would broaden financial inclusion, enabling individuals who have traditionally been excluded from the banking system to participate in these financial activities.

In the realm of international trade, Ripple and XRP could eliminate the long waiting times and high costs typically associated with cross-border payments. Traders could transfer money across borders in real-time, saving precious time and resources.

Furthermore, the role of XRP as a bridge currency could become even more crucial as the adoption of cryptocurrencies increases. As more businesses and individuals start accepting cryptocurrencies, the need for a bridge currency to seamlessly convert one cryptocurrency to another will become paramount. This is where XRP could shine brightly.

The true beauty of Ripple and XRP is the democratization of the financial system that they bring along. They are built on the ethos of an equitable world where everyone, irrespective of their socioeconomic status, has access to quick, inexpensive financial services. With Ripple and XRP, we're not just talking about a new currency or a new technology; we're talking about a world of new possibilities. A world that is exciting, inclusive, and ready for you to explore.

Ripple and XRP's capabilities could extend into sectors such as healthcare, supply chain management, and even digital identity verification.

In healthcare, for instance, Ripple's fast, secure infrastructure could allow for instantaneous transfer of vital health information and medical records across hospitals and countries. This would ensure that regardless of where a patient is, doctors would have immediate access to their medical history, enabling prompt and accurate treatment.

Supply chains could be made more transparent and efficient by using Ripple's technology. The speed of transactions could expedite settlements, while the transparency offered by blockchain could help in tracing a product's journey from start to finish. This could greatly reduce fraud, improve product safety, and increase consumer trust in products.

Ripple's technology could even change how we manage and verify our identities online. Through decentralized identity verification systems built on the Ripple network, individuals could have more control over their personal data, choosing who to share it with, thereby enhancing privacy and security in the digital world.

XRP could also see increased use as a store of value and a medium of exchange. As the adoption of cryptocurrencies broadens, more businesses could begin to accept XRP as payment, increasing its utility and value. Additionally, XRP's role as a bridge currency could be extended to include not just fiat currencies but other cryptocurrencies as well, further enhancing its use case and potential for growth.

Beyond this, the advent of smart contracts on the Ripple network, through platforms like Flare Network, opens up an array of possibilities for automating contracts, creating trustless applications, and more. Developers could leverage this to build a wide variety of decentralized applications that could transform numerous industries.

The potential of Ripple and XRP is not just about redefining transactions; it's about creating a more inclusive, transparent, and efficient global system that touches every aspect of our lives. Whether you're a patient needing urgent medical care overseas, a shopper seeking an easy payment solution, or a farmer wanting to track your produce's journey, Ripple and XRP stand to make life better, simpler, and more rewarding. So buckle up and get ready for an exhilarating ride into a future shaped by Ripple and XRP!

Stepping further into the realm of Ripple and XRP, we see a world where even the fields of law and government could be significantly impacted. Smart contracts on the Ripple network, for instance, could automate and expedite the execution of legal contracts, revolutionizing the legal industry. This would save valuable time and resources, and reduce human error, making the process much more efficient and reliable.

Governmental functions could also see drastic improvements. Ripple's blockchain could help in creating a transparent, immutable record of governmental decisions, reducing corruption and increasing accountability. From tracking public expenditure to maintaining land registry records, Ripple's technology could transform various governmental processes.

Ripple's payment protocol could make it easier for citizens to pay for public services. No more queuing up at government offices to pay taxes or fees. With Ripple and XRP, these payments could be made online, in real-time, making the process much more convenient for citizens and more efficient for the government.

Even the field of energy could be influenced by Ripple and XRP. With the world moving towards greener alternatives, Ripple's energy-efficient blockchain could become a model for future digital currencies and blockchain systems. Unlike Bitcoin and Ethereum, which require significant computational power and energy, the Ripple network achieves consensus without energy-intensive mining, making it a more sustainable choice.

Another fascinating possibility is the development of Decentralized Autonomous Organizations (DAOs) on the Ripple network. DAOs are organizations that are completely run by smart contracts, with no central authority. They allow for democratic decision-making, with members voting on proposals based on their stake in the organization. The transparency and efficiency offered by the Ripple network could make it an ideal platform for building DAOs.

Lastly, Ripple and XRP's potential for driving financial inclusion cannot be overstated. By enabling quick, affordable transactions, they could provide financial services to millions of unbanked or underbanked individuals around the world. This could be life-changing, providing opportunities for economic growth and development in areas where traditional banking systems have failed to reach.

It's a future where technology fuels a more inclusive, transparent, and efficient world. So, whether you're a small business owner, a developer, a government official, or simply someone eager to experience the future of blockchain technology, Ripple and XRP offer a world of opportunities just waiting to be explored!

Emerging from the dawn of a new era in blockchain technology, Ripple and XRP are set to make even larger waves across a myriad of industries, broadening the horizon of what is possible.

In the world of media and entertainment, the transparency and immutability of Ripple's blockchain technology could revolutionize content creation, distribution, and ownership. Artists could leverage the blockchain to create decentralized digital art or music, ensuring that they receive their fair share of profits without intermediaries. Movie studios or game developers could use Ripple for in-app transactions, ensuring fast and secure payments.

Ripple's potential in the realm of education is also significant. Imagine a world where academic credentials are stored on the blockchain, eliminating the risk of fraudulent certificates and making verification a breeze. Universities could even use Ripple's smart contracts to automate the process of awarding scholarships or grading examinations.

In the field of charity and humanitarian aid, Ripple could ensure that donations reach the intended beneficiaries quickly and transparently. By cutting out intermediaries, more of the donated money could go directly to those in need. Furthermore, with the use of smart contracts, aid could be automatically released when certain conditions are met, such as a natural disaster occurring.

Ripple and XRP could also make significant strides in the world of investment and asset management. The high-speed, low-cost transactions enabled by XRP make it an attractive option for institutional investors and hedge funds looking to move large amounts of money quickly and cheaply. Ripple's blockchain could also be used to create and manage a wide range of tokenized assets, from stocks and bonds to real estate and commodities, making investing more accessible to a broader audience.

Cybersecurity becomes increasingly important. Ripple's secure, decentralized network could become a cornerstone in the development of systems and platforms that prioritize data privacy and protection against cyber threats.

Lastly, XRP itself, as a cryptocurrency, could evolve in various ways. It could become a safe-haven asset, similar to how gold is viewed today. As more people begin to understand and trust the stability and utility of XRP, they might start using it as a store of wealth, especially in times of economic uncertainty.

From this vantage point, it's clear that Ripple and XRP are poised to shape our future in ways we can only begin to imagine. Fasten your seatbelts and prepare to journey through the exciting landscape sculpted by Ripple and XRP, where technology, creativity, and innovation harmonize to redefine the contours of our world!

If we gaze even further into the horizon, Ripple and XRP could pioneer astonishing developments in the insurance and gaming industries, and even potentially reshape how we approach voting systems.

The insurance sector, traditionally marred by lengthy claims processes and complex paperwork, could be revolutionized by Ripple's blockchain technology. With smart contracts, claims could be automatically validated and payouts triggered based on predefined conditions. This could lead to a drastic reduction in processing times, providing policyholders with a quicker, more efficient service.

Gaming is another arena where Ripple and XRP could unlock exciting possibilities. The lightning-fast transaction speeds could allow for real-time in-game purchases and trades. Furthermore, Ripple's blockchain could be utilized to create and manage non-fungible tokens (NFTs), unique digital assets that could represent in-game items. This could bring a new level of ownership and tradeability to virtual goods, redefining the economics of gaming.

Moreover, the transparency, security, and immutability provided by Ripple could be leveraged to build secure, tamper-proof voting systems. Votes could be cast and recorded on the blockchain, ensuring that every vote is counted and cannot be altered. This could bring a new level of trust and integrity to elections, making the democratic process more robust and resistant to fraud.

Ripple's technology could also play a vital role in the field of research and development. For instance, scientific research findings could be recorded on the blockchain, establishing an immutable record and discouraging data manipulation. Ripple could also provide a secure platform for sharing and collaborating on research data, catalyzing scientific progress.

Furthermore, XRP's use case could evolve with the advent of new technologies and trends. As the Internet of Things (IoT) expands, XRP could serve as the universal medium of exchange for millions of devices communicating and transacting with each other. Your smart fridge could automatically pay for groceries, or your self-driving car could pay for tolls or charging services — all using XRP.

Ripple and XRP's versatility and scalability make them an ideal foundation for a vast range of applications across numerous sectors. As we move forward, the combination of speed, low transaction costs, and programmability that Ripple and XRP offer could unlock a cascade of transformative use cases. So, buckle up, as we step into an exciting future brimming with endless possibilities in the world of Ripple and XRP!

Consider the impact Ripple could have in the world of employment and human resources. Blockchain-based contracts could replace traditional contracts, providing a secure, immutable, and transparent record of an employee's work agreement. This could help resolve disputes and ensure the fair treatment of employees.

Moreover, in the world of Internet of Things (IoT), where billions of devices are expected to communicate and transact with each other, XRP could serve as the universal medium of exchange. Imagine your car paying for its own parking, or your home automatically purchasing more utilities when running low — all made possible using XRP.

The potential of Ripple in facilitating the development of a shared economy is profound. From shared rides to shared homes, peer-to-peer transactions could be made more secure, transparent, and efficient with Ripple's technology. It could potentially foster trust among users and accelerate the growth of sharing economy platforms.

Additionally, in academia, the blockchain technology underpinning Ripple could be used for secure and transparent record-keeping of academic achievements. Diplomas, certificates, and other accomplishments could be recorded on the blockchain, making them easily verifiable and eliminating the possibility of fraud.

In the realm of public services, blockchain technology can provide an unprecedented level of transparency and efficiency. Government benefits could be distributed to citizens through the blockchain, ensuring that the funds reach the intended recipients without delays or corruption.

Even everyday online shopping could be transformed by Ripple and XRP. With micropayments made possible by XRP, consumers could pay for exactly what they consume — be it an article behind a paywall or a streaming movie they only watch half of.

Imagine the agricultural industry, where Ripple's blockchain could enable the tracking of food from farm to fork. Consumers would know precisely where their food is coming from, increasing transparency and accountability within the food industry. Farmers, on the other hand, could receive prompt payment for their produce via XRP, ensuring they're fairly compensated.

Even our experience of sports and entertainment could be elevated by Ripple's technology. Blockchain-based tickets could prevent fraud and scalping, while smart contracts could automatically handle royalties and copyrights for artists, ensuring they're rightfully rewarded for their work. Moreover, fans could engage with their favorite athletes or artists in novel ways, such as owning tokenized merchandise or unique digital content through non-fungible tokens (NFTs) on the Ripple network.

Further still, Ripple and XRP could play a significant role in the rapidly expanding world of esports and virtual reality. Lightning-fast, low-cost transactions facilitated by XRP could enhance in-game purchases and trades. Gamers could own and trade their virtual assets securely, adding another layer of excitement to the gaming world.

Looking at the bigger picture, Ripple could be instrumental in driving the development of smart cities. Blockchain-based IoT systems could automate various aspects of urban life, from energy management to traffic control, all interconnected via the Ripple network. XRP could serve as the universal currency for these transactions, powering a seamless, efficient urban life.

In terms of personal finance, Ripple could simplify and speed up everything from paying bills to sending money abroad. It could enable instant, low-cost international remittances, giving individuals more control over their money and reducing their dependence on banks. Moreover, the use of XRP as a day-to-day currency could drastically cut transaction times and costs, making it a convenient alternative to traditional fiat currencies.

On a larger scale, Ripple could transform the global remittance industry, which is worth hundreds of billions of dollars. Migrant workers sending money home often face high fees and long wait times. With Ripple and XRP, these remittances could be made almost instantaneously and at a fraction of the cost, making a tangible difference in the lives of millions of people worldwide.

In the retail sector, Ripple's fast and secure payment infrastructure could greatly enhance the customer experience. Imagine buying your favorite products with just a simple click, and the transaction is settled instantly with XRP, regardless of where the retailer is based. This could truly globalize e-commerce, making it faster and more seamless than ever before.

Moreover, Ripple could play a vital role in driving the growth of the digital advertising industry. By using the blockchain to track ad impressions and clicks, Ripple could bring transparency and accountability to digital advertising, ensuring advertisers get what they pay for.

Chapter 1: Introduction to XRP and Ripple

1.1 What is XRP?

XRP is a digital asset or cryptocurrency that operates on the XRP Ledger, a decentralized, open-source blockchain technology. It was created in 2012 by the founders of the technology company Ripple Labs, namely Chris Larsen, Jed McCaleb, and Arthur Britto. XRP was designed to facilitate fast, secure, and cost-efficient cross-border transactions, making it an attractive alternative to traditional payment systems.

In simple terms, XRP is a form of digital money that can be used to transfer value across the internet quickly and inexpensively. Unlike physical cash, XRP exists solely in the digital realm, and its ownership and transactions are recorded on a distributed ledger, meaning the transaction data is stored across multiple computers globally. This decentralized nature ensures that no single entity or government can control or manipulate the XRP Ledger.

XRP serves as the native currency on the XRP Ledger, providing the necessary "fuel" for executing transactions. When a user sends XRP to another user, the transaction is processed and validated by a network of computers, called validators, which work together to reach a consensus on the validity of the transaction. This consensus mechanism allows for efficient and secure processing of transactions without the need for a central authority, like a bank.

The primary goal of XRP is to improve the efficiency and speed of cross-border transactions. Traditional payment systems, such as SWIFT, can be slow, taking several days to complete an international transaction, and may incur high fees. XRP transactions, on the other hand, can be completed within seconds and at a fraction of the cost. This makes XRP particularly appealing to financial institutions and payment providers that need to process a large volume of international transactions.

It is important to note that XRP and Ripple are often used interchangeably, but they are distinct entities. Ripple is the technology company that created XRP and the XRP Ledger, while XRP is the digital asset that operates on the Ledger. Ripple develops and promotes various products and services that leverage the XRP Ledger and XRP to facilitate cross-border transactions, such as RippleNet, a global payment network that connects banks, payment providers, and other financial institutions.

XRP is a digital asset designed to enable fast, secure, and cost-effective cross-border transactions. It operates on the decentralized XRP Ledger, which is maintained by a global network of validators. Ripple, the company behind XRP, has developed various products and services that leverage XRP to improve the efficiency and speed of international payments, making it an increasingly popular option for financial institutions and payment providers.

The journey of Ripple and XRP began in 2004 when Ryan Fugger, a Canadian web developer, conceived the idea of a decentralized digital currency system. Fugger aimed to create a monetary system that allowed individuals to create their own money, ultimately leading to the development of RipplePay, a prototype of a decentralized payment platform launched in 2005.

In 2011, Jed McCaleb, an early Bitcoin enthusiast and the creator of the infamous Mt. Gox cryptocurrency exchange, started to envision a more efficient and scalable alternative to Bitcoin. McCaleb's goal was to develop a digital currency that could address Bitcoin's limitations, such as slow transaction speeds and energy-intensive mining.

To achieve this goal, McCaleb teamed up with Chris Larsen, a successful entrepreneur and the co-founder of several fintech companies, including E-Loan and Prosper. Along with Arthur Britto, a technical expert, they began working on a new digital currency system called OpenCoin. In 2012, OpenCoin developed the XRP Ledger, a decentralized and open-source blockchain technology, and its native digital asset, XRP.

OpenCoin officially rebranded to Ripple Labs Inc. in September 2013, focusing on the development of its payment protocol and the promotion of XRP as a solution for cross-border transactions. Ripple's early days saw investments from high-profile individuals and venture capital firms such as Andreessen Horowitz, Google Ventures, and IDG Capital Partners.

In 2014, Ripple released its first major product, the Ripple Transaction Protocol (RTXP), which later evolved into RippleNet. RippleNet aimed to connect banks, payment providers, and other financial institutions to facilitate faster and more cost-effective cross-border transactions using XRP as a bridge currency.

Throughout its history, Ripple has attracted several influential figures to its executive team and board of directors. In 2015, Brad Garlinghouse, a former executive at AOL and Yahoo!, joined Ripple as the Chief Operating Officer and later became the CEO in 2016. In 2014, Ripple appointed Susan Athey, a renowned economist and professor at Stanford University, to its board of directors.

Over the years, Ripple has formed partnerships with numerous banks and financial institutions across the globe, including Santander, Standard Chartered, American Express, and MoneyGram. These partnerships have showcased Ripple's products' potential to revolutionize the traditional financial system by leveraging XRP's speed, efficiency, and cost-effectiveness.

Despite its successes, Ripple has faced several challenges, including ongoing debates about the decentralization of XRP and a high-profile lawsuit with the U.S. Securities and Exchange Commission (SEC). In December 2020, the SEC filed a lawsuit against Ripple and its executives, alleging that the company had conducted an unregistered securities offering by selling XRP. The legal battle has garnered significant attention from the crypto community and regulators worldwide, and its outcome could have far-reaching implications for XRP's future and the broader cryptocurrency landscape.

The history of Ripple and XRP is marked by continuous innovation and the pursuit of a more efficient global financial system. From its humble beginnings as RipplePay to the development of the XRP Ledger and RippleNet, Ripple has consistently demonstrated its commitment to transforming cross-border transactions. As Ripple continues to forge partnerships and navigate regulatory challenges, the story of XRP and Ripple is far from over.

1.3 The Role of XRP in the Ripple Ecosystem

XRP plays a pivotal role in the Ripple ecosystem, serving as the native digital asset on the XRP Ledger and providing essential functionalities that support Ripple's products and services. The primary objective of XRP is to enable fast, secure, and cost-effective cross-border transactions. To understand XRP's role in the Ripple ecosystem, it is crucial to examine its various functions and how they complement Ripple's broader mission of revolutionizing the global financial system.

Bridge Currency: One of the most significant roles of XRP in the Ripple ecosystem is to serve as a bridge currency for cross-border transactions. In traditional international payments, funds must pass through a complex network of intermediary banks, often involving multiple currency exchanges and resulting in high fees and slow processing times. XRP can act as a bridge between different currencies, allowing financial institutions and payment providers to convert one currency to XRP and then to the target currency in a matter of seconds. This process significantly reduces the costs and complexities associated with traditional correspondent banking systems.

Liquidity Provision: XRP can act as a source of on-demand liquidity for financial institutions using Ripple's products, such as its On-Demand Liquidity (ODL) service, formerly known as xRapid. Traditionally, banks and payment providers must pre-fund nostro and vostro accounts in various jurisdictions to facilitate cross-border transactions, leading to significant capital inefficiencies. By using XRP as a source of on-demand liquidity, financial institutions can eliminate the need for pre-funding and minimize the capital tied up in these accounts, resulting in lower operational costs and improved capital efficiency.

Speed and Scalability: XRP is designed to provide fast and scalable transaction processing, which is critical for the Ripple ecosystem's efficiency. XRP transactions can be confirmed within 3-5 seconds, compared to hours or even days for traditional payment systems or other cryptocurrencies like Bitcoin. Moreover, the XRP Ledger can handle up to 1,500 transactions per second (tps), with the potential for further scalability. This speed and scalability make XRP suitable for handling large volumes of transactions in real-time, a necessary feature for Ripple's financial products and services.

Network Security and Spam Prevention: XRP plays a crucial role in maintaining the security and integrity of the XRP Ledger. To prevent spam and denial-of-service attacks, the XRP Ledger requires a small transaction fee, which is paid in XRP. These fees are minimal (typically a fraction of a cent), but they deter malicious actors from flooding the network with spam transactions. The collected fees are destroyed, reducing the overall XRP supply and preventing inflationary pressures.

Decentralized Exchange (DEX): The XRP Ledger incorporates a built-in decentralized exchange, allowing users to trade various digital assets directly on the ledger without relying on a centralized exchange. XRP serves as the base currency for trading on this decentralized exchange, facilitating efficient and secure asset exchange within the Ripple ecosystem.

XRP is an integral component of the Ripple ecosystem, providing essential functionalities that support Ripple's products and services. As a bridge currency, source of on-demand liquidity, and facilitator of fast, secure, and scalable transactions, XRP plays a critical role in realizing Ripple's vision of revolutionizing the global financial system.

XRP, like other cryptocurrencies, is a digital asset designed to enable secure and decentralized transactions. However, it possesses distinct features and characteristics that set it apart from other major cryptocurrencies such as Bitcoin (BTC), Ethereum (ETH), and Litecoin (LTC). In this section, we will compare XRP to other cryptocurrencies, highlighting the key differences, pros, and cons.

Transaction Speed and Scalability:
Pros: XRP is known for its remarkably fast transaction speeds, with confirmation times ranging between 3-5 seconds. This is a significant advantage over Bitcoin (10 minutes), Ethereum (15 seconds to a few minutes), and Litecoin (2.5 minutes). Moreover, XRP can handle up to 1,500 transactions per second (tps), which is considerably higher than Bitcoin (3-7 tps), Ethereum (15-45 tps), and Litecoin (56 tps). This speed and scalability make XRP suitable for large-scale financial systems and real-time transaction processing.
Cons: Some newer cryptocurrencies and blockchain platforms, such as Solana and Algorand, boast even faster transaction speeds and higher throughput. However, these platforms have not been battle-tested to the same extent as the XRP Ledger.
Consensus Mechanism:
Pros: Unlike Bitcoin, Ethereum, and Litecoin, which rely on energy-intensive Proof of Work (PoW) mining, XRP utilizes a consensus mechanism called the Ripple Protocol Consensus Algorithm (RPCA). The RPCA allows a network

of validators to agree on the validity of transactions without the need for mining, making the XRP Ledger more energy-efficient and environmentally friendly. The RPCA also helps maintain the network's security without the risk of a 51% attack, which is a concern for PoW-based cryptocurrencies.

Cons: Critics argue that the RPCA is less decentralized than PoW or Proof of Stake (PoS) consensus mechanisms, as it relies on a limited set of trusted validators. However, Ripple has been working to increase the decentralization of the XRP Ledger by adding more diverse and independent validators.

Use Case and Utility:

Pros: XRP is specifically designed for cross-border transactions, providing a focused use case that directly addresses the inefficiencies of traditional financial systems. Its role as a bridge currency and a source of on-demand liquidity sets it apart from cryptocurrencies like Bitcoin, which primarily serve as a store of value or digital gold, and Ethereum, which is a platform for decentralized applications (dApps) and smart contracts. This focus on a specific use case has allowed Ripple to tailor its products and services to the needs of banks, payment providers, and financial institutions.

Cons: XRP's specialized use case may limit its broader appeal, as it does not encompass the diverse range of applications and functionalities offered by platforms like Ethereum.

Market Capitalization and Adoption:

Pros: XRP has consistently ranked among the top cryptocurrencies by market capitalization, demonstrating its sustained popularity and investor confidence. Its adoption by numerous banks, payment providers, and financial institutions showcases its potential to revolutionize cross-border transactions and make a meaningful impact on the global financial system.

Cons: XRP's market capitalization and adoption are still lower than those of Bitcoin and Ethereum, which have gained more widespread recognition and acceptance.

Regulatory Status:

Pros: Ripple has been actively engaging with regulators and policymakers worldwide to promote a clear and supportive regulatory environment for XRP and other digital assets.

Cons: The ongoing SEC lawsuit against Ripple has raised questions about XRP's regulatory status, specifically whether it should be classified as a security, currency, or commodity. This legal battle has led to uncertainty about XRP's future in the U.S. market, with some exchanges delisting or suspending XRP trading until the matter is resolved. While the outcome of the lawsuit remains uncertain, it could have far-reaching implications for XRP's future and the broader cryptocurrency landscape.

XRP possesses distinct advantages and disadvantages compared to other cryptocurrencies. Its speed, scalability, and energy efficiency set it apart from Bitcoin, Ethereum, and Litecoin, making it well-suited for cross-border transactions and large-scale financial systems. However, XRP faces challenges in terms of decentralization, regulatory uncertainty, and competition from newer cryptocurrencies with even faster transaction speeds. Understanding these key differences is crucial for investors, financial institutions, and users to make informed decisions about XRP and its role in the broader cryptocurrency ecosystem.

The XRP Ledger is a decentralized, open-source blockchain technology that underpins XRP, the digital asset designed for fast and cost-effective cross-border transactions. The XRP Ledger is maintained by a global network of validators that work together to achieve consensus on the validity of transactions, ensuring the security and integrity of the ledger. In this section, we will explore the fundamental components and features of the XRP Ledger, providing a comprehensive understanding of its inner workings.

Consensus Mechanism: The XRP Ledger employs a unique consensus mechanism called the Ripple Protocol Consensus Algorithm (RPCA). Unlike Proof of Work (PoW) or Proof of Stake (PoS) mechanisms used by many other cryptocurrencies, the RPCA relies on a network of validators that reach consensus on the state of the ledger. Validators propose and validate transactions, and a supermajority (typically 80% or more) must agree on the transaction set for it to be considered valid. This consensus process occurs every 3-5 seconds, resulting in fast and secure transaction confirmations.

Validators: Validators are essential participants in the XRP Ledger, responsible for maintaining the network's security and ensuring transaction validity. Validators can be run by various entities, including businesses, financial institutions, or individuals, and are not compensated for their work. Ripple has been actively working to increase the decentralization of the XRP Ledger by adding more independent and diverse validators to the network. The validator's trustworthiness is determined by the Unique Node List (UNL), a list of reputable validators that users can choose to trust.

Accounts: The XRP Ledger uses account-based data structures instead of the unspent transaction output (UTXO) model employed by Bitcoin. Each account on the XRP Ledger has a unique address, a cryptographic public key, and a corresponding private key. Accounts store XRP balances, manage trust lines, and define transaction settings. To create an account, a user must deposit a minimum amount of XRP, known as the reserve requirement, which helps prevent spam and malicious account creation.

Transaction Fees and Reserves: The XRP Ledger requires a small transaction fee, paid in XRP, to prevent spam and denial-of-service attacks. Transaction fees are minimal (typically a fraction of a cent) and are destroyed after being collected, reducing the overall XRP supply and preventing inflation. Additionally, the XRP Ledger imposes reserve requirements for creating accounts and maintaining trust lines, ensuring that users have a stake in the network and discouraging malicious behavior.

Cryptographic Security: The XRP Ledger employs cryptographic algorithms such as the Elliptic Curve Digital Signature Algorithm (ECDSA) and the Ed25519 signature scheme to ensure transaction security and user privacy.

These cryptographic methods allow users to sign transactions with their private keys, proving ownership of their accounts without revealing sensitive information. Decentralized Exchange (DEX): The XRP Ledger incorporates a built-in decentralized exchange that enables users to trade various digital assets directly on the ledger. Users can create and manage offers to buy or sell assets, with XRP serving as the base currency for trading pairs. The DEX allows for secure, trustless, and efficient asset exchange without relying on centralized platforms.

Issued Currencies and Trust Lines: The XRP Ledger supports the issuance and trading of custom digital assets or "IOUs," representing any form of value, such as fiat currencies, cryptocurrencies, or commodities. Users can create trust lines with other accounts to extend or receive credit, enabling the issuance and trading of these custom assets. Trust lines help facilitate the decentralized exchange of value and enhance the utility of the XRP Ledger.

The XRP Ledger is a powerful and innovative blockchain technology designed to enable fast, secure, and cost-effective cross-border transactions. Its unique consensus mechanism, decentralized exchange, and support for issued currencies make it a versatile platform for a wide range of financial applications. By understanding the fundamental components and features of the XRP Ledger, users can better appreciate its potential to revolutionize the global financial system and drive the adoption of digital assets.

2.2 Consensus Protocol and the Ripple Protocol Consensus Algorithm (RPCA)

Consensus protocols are crucial for maintaining the integrity and security of decentralized blockchain networks. They are the processes by which participants in the network agree on the validity of transactions and the state of the blockchain. In this section, we will explain the Ripple Protocol Consensus Algorithm (RPCA), the unique consensus mechanism used by the XRP Ledger, in a manner that is accessible to non-technical readers.

The Ripple Protocol Consensus Algorithm (RPCA) is a consensus mechanism that relies on a network of validators to reach agreement on the state of the XRP Ledger. Unlike Proof of Work (PoW) or Proof of Stake (PoS) mechanisms, which depend on mining or staking for transaction validation, the RPCA uses a more energy-efficient and scalable approach.

The RPCA process can be broken down into several steps:

Candidate Set Formation: Validators on the XRP Ledger continuously monitor incoming transactions and collect them into a set called the "candidate set." This set represents all the transactions that the validators have seen and deem valid but have not yet been added to the ledger. Proposal Round: In this phase, each validator proposes its candidate set to other validators in the network. Validators share their candidate sets with one another to compare the transactions they have seen and to ensure they are working with the same information.

Voting: Validators vote on the transactions in the candidate sets they have received from other validators. If a validator sees that a supermajority (typically 80% or more) of other validators agree on a specific transaction, it will include that transaction in its next proposal. Validators may need to go through several rounds of voting, each time narrowing down the set of transactions until they reach a consensus.

Ledger Closure: Once a supermajority of validators agree on the same set of transactions, the consensus process is considered complete. The agreed-upon transactions are then added to the ledger as a new "ledger version." The ledger is updated, and the process starts again for the next round of transactions.

The RPCA offers several advantages over PoW or PoS mechanisms:

Speed: The RPCA can reach consensus in just 3-5 seconds, resulting in faster transaction confirmations compared to Bitcoin (10 minutes) or Ethereum (15 seconds to a few minutes).

Energy Efficiency: Since the RPCA does not require mining or staking, it consumes significantly less energy, making it more environmentally friendly and sustainable.

Scalability: The RPCA can handle a higher transaction throughput (up to 1,500 transactions per second) than PoW or PoS mechanisms, enabling it to support large-scale financial systems and real-time transaction processing.

Security: The RPCA helps maintain the network's security without the risk of a 51% attack, which is a concern for PoW-based cryptocurrencies.

However, the RPCA has faced criticism regarding its decentralization, as it relies on a limited set of trusted validators. To address this concern, Ripple has been working to increase the decentralization of the XRP Ledger by adding more diverse and independent validators.

The Ripple Protocol Consensus Algorithm (RPCA) is a unique consensus mechanism that enables fast, secure, and energy-efficient transaction processing on the XRP Ledger. By understanding the fundamental concepts and steps involved in the RPCA, non-technical users can better appreciate the innovation and potential of the XRP Ledger in revolutionizing the global financial system.

2.3 Transactions and Fees on the XRP Ledger

The XRP Ledger enables users to perform various types of transactions, such as sending XRP, trading assets on the decentralized exchange, and managing trust lines. To maintain the network's security and prevent spam or denial-of-service attacks, the XRP Ledger imposes small transaction fees. In this section, we will provide a comprehensive explanation of transactions and fees on the XRP Ledger, ensuring that the concepts are accessible to non-technical readers.

Types of Transactions: The XRP Ledger supports several types of transactions, including:

Payment: Sending XRP or issued currencies (IOUs) between accounts.

OfferCreate: Placing an order on the decentralized exchange to buy or sell assets.

OfferCancel: Canceling an existing order on the decentralized exchange.

TrustSet: Establishing or modifying a trust line between accounts, allowing users to extend or receive credit for issued currencies.

AccountSet: Modifying an account's settings, such as the transfer rate or account flags.

Escrow: Creating, executing, or canceling an escrow transaction, which locks up XRP until specific conditions are met.

Transaction Fees: To submit a transaction to the XRP Ledger, users must pay a small transaction fee in XRP. This fee serves several purposes:

Discouraging Spam: The transaction fee helps prevent the network from being overwhelmed by spam or malicious transactions, as attackers would need to spend significant amounts of XRP to flood the network.

Prioritizing Transactions: In times of high network congestion, transaction fees act as a market-driven mechanism to prioritize transactions. Users can choose to pay higher fees to ensure their transactions are processed faster.

Maintaining Security: Requiring transaction fees helps maintain the XRP Ledger's security by creating a cost for potential attackers, making it more challenging to disrupt the network.

Calculation: Transaction fees on the XRP Ledger are determined by a base fee, which is multiplied by the transaction's "load cost." The base fee is the minimum cost for a transaction (currently set at 0.00001 XRP), while the load cost is a factor that increases during periods of high network activity to prioritize transactions. Users can choose to pay higher fees to increase the likelihood of their transaction being processed quickly during times of congestion. It is important to note that transaction fees are not paid to validators or any other party; instead, they are destroyed, reducing the overall XRP supply and preventing inflation.

Reserves: In addition to transaction fees, the XRP Ledger also enforces reserve requirements for accounts and trust lines. These reserves are designed to prevent spam and ensure that users have a stake in the network. To create an account on the XRP Ledger, a user must deposit a minimum amount of XRP, known as the "base reserve" (currently set at 20 XRP). Similarly, establishing a trust line requires an "owner reserve" (currently set at 5 XRP). These reserves are not destroyed or paid to any party; they remain in the user's account and can be recovered if the account is deleted or the trust line is closed.

The XRP Ledger enables various types of transactions to facilitate digital asset management and exchange. Transaction fees and reserves serve to maintain the network's security, prevent spam, and ensure smooth operation during periods of high activity. By understanding the role and structure of transactions and fees on the XRP Ledger, non-technical users can better appreciate its efficiency and potential to revolutionize the global financial system.

2.4 Validators and Unique Node Lists

Validators and Unique Node Lists (UNLs) play essential roles in maintaining the XRP Ledger's security, integrity, and decentralization. Validators are responsible for proposing and validating transactions, while UNLs represent a list of trusted validators. In this section, we will provide a comprehensive explanation of validators and Unique Node Lists, ensuring that these concepts are accessible to non-technical readers.

Validators: Validators are nodes on the XRP Ledger network that participate in the consensus process. They are responsible for verifying transactions and maintaining the ledger's security and integrity. Validators propose transactions, share their candidate sets with other validators, and vote on the validity of transactions. Validators can be run by various entities, such as businesses, financial institutions, or individuals, and they are not compensated for their work on the network. The more diverse and independent validators there are on the network, the more decentralized and secure the XRP Ledger becomes.

Unique Node Lists (UNLs): The Unique Node List (UNL) is a curated list of trusted validators that each participant on the XRP Ledger chooses to rely on for transaction validation. When a user submits a transaction, their node consults the validators in its UNL to determine if the transaction is valid. A transaction is considered valid if a supermajority (typically 80% or more) of validators on a user's UNL agree on its validity.

Importance of UNLs: UNLs play a crucial role in maintaining the XRP Ledger's security and decentralization. By allowing users to choose their own set of trusted validators, the XRP Ledger ensures that no single entity can control the network or manipulate transaction validation. This decentralization helps maintain the network's security and makes it more resistant to attacks or censorship.

Selecting a UNL: Users can select their UNL based on various factors, such as reputation, performance, and geographic location. Ripple, the company behind the XRP Ledger, provides a default UNL that includes a diverse set of reputable validators. However, users are free to create their own UNL or modify the default list to suit their needs. It is important to carefully select a UNL, as relying on untrustworthy validators could compromise the security and integrity of a user's transactions.

Decentralization Efforts: Critics have raised concerns about the XRP Ledger's decentralization due to the influence of Ripple and its default UNL. In response, Ripple has been actively working to increase the number of independent and diverse validators on the network, reducing the company's influence and promoting a more decentralized ecosystem.

Validators and Unique Node Lists are vital components of the XRP Ledger, ensuring the network's security, integrity, and decentralization. Validators participate in the consensus process, while UNLs represent curated lists of trusted validators. By understanding the roles and importance of validators and UNLs, non-technical users can better appreciate the XRP Ledger's potential to revolutionize the global financial system while maintaining a secure and decentralized infrastructure.

Chapter 3: The RippleNet and Its Impact
3.1 Introduction to RippleNet

RippleNet is a global payment network developed by Ripple, the company behind the XRP Ledger and XRP cryptocurrency. It aims to revolutionize cross-border transactions by providing financial institutions with a fast, secure, and cost-effective solution for processing international payments. RippleNet leverages the power of blockchain technology and digital assets, like XRP, to enable real-time settlements and improve the overall efficiency of the global financial system. In this section, we will provide a comprehensive explanation of RippleNet, ensuring that the concepts are accessible to a non-technical audience.

Purpose of RippleNet: The primary goal of RippleNet is to address the inefficiencies and high costs associated with traditional cross-border payment systems. Currently, international payments rely on the outdated SWIFT system, which involves multiple intermediaries, slow transaction times, and high fees. RippleNet offers an alternative solution by using blockchain technology and digital assets to facilitate direct, real-time settlements between financial institutions, reducing transaction times and costs.

Components of RippleNet: RippleNet is comprised of several components that work together to enable seamless cross-border transactions. These components include:

xCurrent: xCurrent is a messaging system that allows financial institutions to communicate and coordinate the processing of cross-border payments in real-time. It provides end-to-end transaction tracking, ensuring transparency and reducing the risk of errors.

xRapid (now known as On-Demand Liquidity or ODL): xRapid is a liquidity solution that leverages XRP to enable real-time cross-border settlements. By using XRP as a bridge currency, financial institutions can eliminate the need for pre-funded nostro/vostro accounts, reducing capital requirements and lowering operational costs.

xVia: xVia is a standardized API (Application Programming Interface) that allows businesses and payment providers to send cross-border payments through RippleNet easily. It simplifies the integration process and provides a consistent user experience across different networks and geographies.

Benefits of RippleNet: RippleNet offers several advantages over traditional cross-border payment systems, including:

Speed: RippleNet enables real-time settlements, significantly reducing transaction times from days to just a few seconds.

Cost Savings: By streamlining the payment process and eliminating intermediaries, RippleNet reduces transaction fees and operational costs for financial institutions.

Transparency: RippleNet provides end-to-end transaction tracking, ensuring that all parties have visibility into the status of a payment and reducing the risk of errors or delays.

Accessibility: RippleNet connects banks, payment providers, and businesses worldwide, making it easier for them to process cross-border payments and access new markets.

Adoption and Impact: Since its launch, RippleNet has attracted over 300 financial institutions, including banks, payment providers, and remittance companies, to join its network. By providing a faster, more cost-effective solution for international payments, RippleNet has the potential to improve financial inclusion, promote global trade, and drive economic growth in various parts of the world.

RippleNet is a global payment network that aims to revolutionize cross-border transactions by leveraging blockchain technology and digital assets like XRP. By offering a faster, more secure, and cost-effective alternative to traditional payment systems, RippleNet has the potential to significantly impact the global financial landscape and improve the lives of millions of people worldwide. By understanding the purpose, components, and benefits of RippleNet, non-technical users can better appreciate its potential to drive innovation and positive change in the world of finance.

RippleNet, the global payment network developed by Ripple, is built upon three core components or "pillars": xCurrent, xRapid (now known as On-Demand Liquidity or ODL), and xVia. Each of these pillars serves a specific purpose and contributes to the overall efficiency and effectiveness of the network. In this section, we will provide a comprehensive explanation of the three pillars of RippleNet, ensuring that the concepts are accessible to a non-technical audience.

xCurrent: xCurrent is a messaging and settlement system designed to facilitate real-time communication and coordination between financial institutions for cross-border payments. It operates using Ripple's Interledger Protocol (ILP), which enables secure and instant transfer of funds between different ledgers and networks. xCurrent offers several benefits, including:

Real-time communication: xCurrent allows banks and payment providers to exchange information about a transaction instantly, ensuring that all parties are aware of the payment's status and details.

Atomic settlements: xCurrent enables simultaneous and instant settlement of transactions, reducing the risk of errors or delays in the payment process.

Compliance and risk management: xCurrent supports a range of compliance and risk management features, such as sanctions screening and transaction monitoring, ensuring that cross-border payments meet regulatory requirements.

xRapid (On-Demand Liquidity): xRapid, now known as On-Demand Liquidity (ODL), is a liquidity solution that leverages XRP as a bridge currency to enable real-time cross-border settlements. By utilizing XRP, ODL addresses the issue of pre-funded nostro/vostro accounts, which are traditionally required for international payments. This leads to several benefits, such as:

Reduced capital requirements: ODL eliminates the need for banks and payment providers to maintain pre-funded accounts in multiple currencies, freeing up capital for other uses.

Lower costs: By using XRP to facilitate cross-border transactions, ODL reduces the costs associated with currency exchange and international payment processing. Faster settlements: ODL allows for real-time settlements, significantly reducing transaction times compared to traditional payment systems.

xVia: xVia is a standardized API (Application Programming Interface) that enables businesses, payment providers, and other users to send cross-border payments through RippleNet quickly and easily. xVia simplifies the integration process and provides a consistent user experience across different networks and geographies. The benefits of xVia include:

Easy integration: xVia's standardized API makes it easy for businesses and payment providers to connect with RippleNet and access its features without extensive technical knowledge or development work.

Consistent user experience: xVia ensures that users have a uniform experience when sending cross-border payments, regardless of the network or geography involved. Enhanced payment tracking: xVia provides end-to-end payment tracking, improving transparency and reducing the risk of errors or delays in the payment process.

The three pillars of RippleNet – xCurrent, xRapid (On-Demand Liquidity), and xVia – work together to create a fast, secure, and cost-effective solution for cross-border payments. By providing real-time communication, instant settlements, and easy integration, RippleNet has the potential to revolutionize the global financial system and improve the lives of millions of people worldwide. By understanding the roles and benefits of xCurrent, xRapid (ODL), and xVia, non-technical users can better appreciate the impact of RippleNet on the world of finance.

3.3 RippleNet's Adoption in the Banking and Finance Industry

The RippleNet payment network has garnered significant interest and adoption in the banking and finance industry. Its ability to provide fast, secure, and cost-effective cross-border payment solutions makes it an attractive alternative to traditional payment systems. In this section, we will discuss the adoption of RippleNet by various financial institutions and the implications for the industry as a whole.

Growing Network of Partners: Since its inception, RippleNet has attracted over 300 financial institutions, including major banks, payment providers, and remittance companies, to join its network. Some notable partners include American Express, Santander, Standard Chartered, SBI Remit, and MoneyGram. By partnering with RippleNet, these institutions can offer their customers faster and more affordable international payment services.

Use Cases and Success Stories: RippleNet's partners have successfully implemented its solutions to improve their cross-border payment processes. For instance, Santander launched One Pay FX, a mobile app powered by RippleNet, which enables customers to make international payments in real-time. Similarly, Standard Chartered employed RippleNet's technology to improve its cross-border payment services, reducing transaction times from two days to just 10 seconds. These success stories demonstrate

RippleNet's potential to transform the way financial institutions conduct international transactions.

RippleNet's Impact on the SWIFT System: RippleNet's growing adoption poses a challenge to the traditional SWIFT system, which currently handles most cross-border payments. As more financial institutions join RippleNet and adopt its solutions, the SWIFT system may face increased competition and pressure to innovate. RippleNet's success could ultimately drive the development of more efficient, secure, and cost-effective payment systems within the banking and finance industry.

Regulatory Considerations: The adoption of RippleNet and other blockchain-based payment solutions has also raised regulatory concerns. Financial institutions must ensure that their use of RippleNet complies with relevant regulations, such as Anti-Money Laundering (AML) and Know Your

Customer (KYC) requirements. Ripple has been working closely with regulators and industry stakeholders to ensure its solutions meet these standards and foster a favorable regulatory environment for digital assets and blockchain technology.

Future Prospects: The growing adoption of RippleNet in the banking and finance industry signals a shift towards more efficient and innovative payment systems. As blockchain technology and digital assets like XRP continue to mature, we can expect to see further adoption and integration of RippleNet's solutions by financial institutions worldwide. This could ultimately lead to a more interconnected and efficient global financial system, benefiting businesses, consumers, and economies alike.

RippleNet's adoption in the banking and finance industry has been steadily increasing, driven by its ability to provide faster, more secure, and cost-effective cross-border payment solutions. With a growing network of partners and numerous success stories, RippleNet has the potential to reshape the way financial institutions conduct international transactions and drive innovation within the industry.

3.4 RippleNet's Advantages over Traditional Payment Systems

RippleNet, the global payment network developed by Ripple, offers several key advantages over traditional payment systems, particularly in the realm of cross-border transactions. In this section, we will explore the benefits of RippleNet in comparison to conventional methods such as the SWIFT system, which currently dominates international payments.

Speed: One of the most significant advantages of RippleNet is its ability to facilitate real-time cross-border settlements. Traditional payment systems like SWIFT often take several days to process international transactions, leading to delays and increased costs. RippleNet's technology, on the other hand, enables instant settlements, reducing transaction times from days to just a few seconds.

Cost Savings: RippleNet offers a more cost-effective solution for processing international payments. Traditional payment systems involve multiple intermediaries, each of which may charge fees for their services. By using blockchain technology and digital assets like XRP to streamline the payment process, RippleNet can significantly reduce transaction fees and operational costs for financial institutions.

Transparency: RippleNet provides end-to-end transaction tracking, ensuring that all parties involved in a payment have visibility into its status and details. This level of transparency is not typically available in traditional payment systems, which can make it difficult for banks and payment providers to track and verify transactions. Improved transparency reduces the risk of errors, delays, and disputes in the payment process.

Elimination of Pre-Funding: In traditional payment systems, banks and payment providers need to maintain pre-funded nostro/vostro accounts in multiple currencies to facilitate cross-border transactions. This practice ties up significant amounts of capital and can lead to currency risk.

RippleNet's On-Demand Liquidity (ODL) solution, which leverages XRP as a bridge currency, eliminates the need for pre-funded accounts, reducing capital requirements and lowering operational costs.

Accessibility: RippleNet connects banks, payment providers, and businesses worldwide, making it easier for them to process cross-border payments and access new markets. In contrast, traditional payment systems may have limited reach, particularly in developing countries or regions with less developed financial infrastructure. By providing a more accessible solution, RippleNet has the potential to improve financial inclusion and promote global trade.

Security: Blockchain technology, which underpins RippleNet, offers a high level of security for financial transactions. The distributed nature of the blockchain makes it resistant to hacking and fraud, ensuring that payment information is secure and protected. Traditional payment systems may be more vulnerable to cyberattacks or data breaches, which can compromise the integrity of the payment process.

RippleNet's advantages over traditional payment systems include faster transaction speeds, reduced costs, increased transparency, elimination of pre-funding requirements, greater accessibility, and enhanced security. By offering a more efficient and innovative solution for cross-border payments, RippleNet has the potential to revolutionize the global financial landscape and improve the lives of millions of people worldwide.

Chapter 4: XRP Use Cases and Applications

4.1 Cross-Border Payments and Remittances

One of the primary use cases and applications of XRP, the native digital asset of the XRP Ledger, is in facilitating cross-border payments and remittances. In this section, we will explore how XRP can improve the efficiency, speed, and cost of international transactions for individuals, businesses, and financial institutions.

Faster Transactions: Cross-border payments and remittances conducted through traditional systems, such as SWIFT, can take several days to process. This can be problematic for individuals and businesses that rely on timely transactions, especially in cases of emergencies or time-sensitive matters. XRP, on the other hand, enables near-instant transaction settlement, with payments typically taking just a few seconds to complete. This increased speed can be a game-changer for international transactions, allowing users to send and receive funds quickly and efficiently.

Lower Costs: Traditional cross-border payment systems often involve multiple intermediaries, each of which may charge fees for their services. This can result in high costs for individuals and businesses making international transactions. XRP's ability to act as a bridge currency in cross-border payments, coupled with the low transaction fees on the XRP Ledger, can significantly reduce the costs associated with international transactions. This cost reduction can benefit both the sender and the receiver, making cross-border payments more affordable and accessible.

Currency Exchange: When sending funds internationally, users often need to convert their native currency into the recipient's currency. This process can be complex and may involve additional fees and unfavorable exchange rates. XRP can streamline this process by acting as a bridge currency, enabling seamless currency exchange and reducing the friction associated with traditional currency conversions.

Improved Access and Financial Inclusion: XRP and the RippleNet payment network can help improve access to cross-border payment services, particularly in regions with less developed financial infrastructure or limited access to traditional banking services. By enabling faster, more affordable, and secure international transactions, XRP can contribute to greater financial inclusion and promote economic growth in underserved areas.

Enhanced Security: The XRP Ledger's consensus mechanism and cryptographic security features help ensure the integrity and safety of transactions. This level of security can offer users peace of mind when sending and receiving funds across borders, reducing the risks associated with fraud and cyberattacks.

XRP's role in cross-border payments and remittances offers significant advantages over traditional payment systems. By enabling faster transactions, lower costs, streamlined currency exchange, improved access, and enhanced security, XRP has the potential to revolutionize the way individuals, businesses, and financial institutions conduct international transactions.

4.2 Liquidity Provisioning for Financial Institutions

Liquidity provisioning is a critical aspect of financial institutions' operations, as it enables them to facilitate various transactions and meet their clients' needs. XRP, as a digital asset, can play a crucial role in providing liquidity for financial institutions, offering several benefits over traditional methods. In this section, we will explore how XRP can be used for liquidity provisioning and the advantages it offers to financial institutions.

On-Demand Liquidity (ODL): One of the primary ways XRP can be used for liquidity provisioning is through Ripple's On-Demand Liquidity (ODL) service. ODL leverages XRP as a bridge currency, allowing financial institutions to source liquidity instantly, without the need for pre-funded nostro/vostro accounts. By using XRP to facilitate cross-border transactions, financial institutions can access liquidity on demand, improving their operational efficiency and reducing costs.

Reduced Capital Requirements: Traditional liquidity provisioning methods often involve maintaining pre-funded accounts in multiple currencies, tying up significant amounts of capital. With XRP and ODL, financial institutions can eliminate the need for these pre-funded accounts, freeing up capital for other uses. This can lead to improved balance sheet management and better allocation of resources within the institution.

Cost Savings: By utilizing XRP for liquidity provisioning, financial institutions can save on transaction fees and operational costs. As mentioned earlier, XRP transactions are fast and have low fees, making them an attractive option for institutions looking to optimize their liquidity management. Additionally, the elimination of pre-funded accounts can result in substantial cost savings related to maintaining and managing these accounts.

Market Making Opportunities: XRP's growing adoption and market presence create opportunities for financial institutions to participate in market making activities. Institutions can leverage their expertise in trading and risk management to facilitate XRP-based transactions, earning profits from bid-ask spreads and providing additional liquidity to the market. This can lead to new revenue streams and increased profitability for financial institutions.

Diversification: Using XRP for liquidity provisioning allows financial institutions to diversify their sources of liquidity, reducing reliance on traditional banking systems and correspondent banks. This diversification can help institutions mitigate risks associated with single points of failure and improve their overall resilience in the face of market fluctuations or disruptions.

XRP offers significant benefits for liquidity provisioning in financial institutions, including on-demand liquidity, reduced capital requirements, cost savings, market-making opportunities, and diversification. By leveraging XRP as a tool for liquidity management, financial institutions can improve their operational efficiency, reduce costs, and enhance their resilience in an ever-evolving financial landscape.

4.3 Micropayments and Web Monetization

Micropayments and web monetization are emerging use cases for digital assets like XRP, offering new ways for individuals and businesses to transact and monetize their online content. In this section, we will explore how XRP can facilitate micropayments and enable web monetization, making it easier for content creators to earn revenue and for users to access digital services.

Low Transaction Fees: One of the main challenges with micropayments has been the high transaction fees associated with traditional payment systems. These fees can make small transactions impractical or uneconomical. XRP, with its low transaction fees, can make micropayments more viable, enabling small transactions for digital services, such as accessing premium content, tipping, or making in-app purchases.

Speed: Another advantage of using XRP for micropayments is its fast transaction settlement. Traditional payment systems can take several seconds or even minutes to process a transaction, which can be a barrier for instant access to digital services. With XRP, transactions are typically settled within a few seconds, providing users with seamless and frictionless access to content and services.

Web Monetization: XRP can be used as part of web monetization solutions, such as Coil, which allow content creators to earn revenue directly from their audience. With Coil, users can subscribe to a monthly plan, and their payments are automatically distributed to content creators based on the amount of time spent consuming their content. This system leverages XRP's fast and low-cost transactions to enable a more equitable and efficient revenue-sharing model, benefiting both creators and consumers.

Simplified Payments: Integrating XRP into micropayment and web monetization platforms can simplify the payment process for users. For instance, using digital wallets or browser extensions, users can seamlessly pay for content or services without the need for complicated payment setups or lengthy registration processes. This ease of use can help drive the adoption of micropayments and web monetization, benefiting both content creators and users.

Global Accessibility: XRP's borderless nature makes it an ideal currency for micropayments and web monetization, as it allows users and content creators to transact seamlessly across different countries and currencies. This global accessibility can help break down barriers to content consumption and enable more equitable access to digital services and information.

XRP offers several advantages for micropayments and web monetization, including low transaction fees, fast settlement, simplified payments, and global accessibility. By leveraging XRP in these use cases, content creators can develop new revenue streams, users can access digital services more easily, and the online ecosystem can evolve toward a more equitable and efficient model.

4.4 Decentralized Finance (DeFi) and XRP

Decentralized Finance (DeFi) refers to a range of financial services and applications built on blockchain technology that operates without the need for traditional intermediaries like banks or financial institutions. XRP, as a digital asset, can play an essential role in the DeFi ecosystem, offering various benefits and opportunities. In this section, we will explore the potential applications and impact of XRP within the DeFi landscape.

Increased Efficiency: XRP's fast transaction settlement times and low fees make it well-suited for various DeFi applications, such as lending, borrowing, or trading. By leveraging XRP in these use cases, users can enjoy more efficient and cost-effective financial services compared to traditional systems.

Interoperability: XRP's ability to act as a bridge currency can facilitate interoperability between different blockchains and DeFi platforms. This capability can enable seamless cross-chain transactions, enhancing the overall user experience and promoting greater collaboration within the DeFi ecosystem.

Liquidity Provision: As mentioned earlier, XRP can provide on-demand liquidity for financial institutions, a feature that can also benefit the DeFi space. By using XRP as a source of liquidity, DeFi platforms can reduce the barriers to entry for users, making it easier for them to participate in various financial services like lending, borrowing, or staking.

Collateralization: XRP can also be used as collateral in DeFi applications, allowing users to take out loans or participate in yield-generating activities. By offering XRP as collateral, users can unlock additional value from their digital assets and access new financial opportunities within the DeFi ecosystem.

Decentralized Exchanges (DEXs) and Trading: XRP can be integrated into decentralized exchanges (DEXs) and trading platforms, enabling users to trade XRP for other digital assets or fiat currencies without relying on centralized intermediaries. This can lead to increased financial freedom, reduced counterparty risk, and a more inclusive financial ecosystem.

Smart Contracts and Decentralized Applications (dApps): While the XRP Ledger does not natively support smart contracts, platforms like Flare Network enable the use of XRP with smart contracts and decentralized applications (dApps) in the DeFi space. This integration can further expand XRP's potential within the DeFi ecosystem, opening up new use cases and opportunities for both developers and users.

XRP has the potential to play a significant role in the DeFi landscape, offering increased efficiency, interoperability, liquidity provision, collateralization, and integration with DEXs, smart contracts, and dApps. By leveraging XRP within the DeFi ecosystem, users can access a more inclusive, decentralized, and efficient financial system, promoting financial freedom and innovation.

Chapter 5: Investing in XRP
5.1 How to Buy and Store XRP

Investing in XRP involves purchasing the digital asset and securely storing it. In this section, we will guide you through the process of buying and storing XRP, ensuring that you understand the necessary steps even if you're new to the world of cryptocurrencies.

Choose a Cryptocurrency Exchange: To buy XRP, you will first need to choose a cryptocurrency exchange. These exchanges are platforms where you can buy, sell, and trade various cryptocurrencies, including XRP. Some popular exchanges that support XRP include Binance, Coinbase, Bitstamp, and Kraken. When selecting an exchange, consider factors such as fees, security, available trading pairs, and ease of use.

Create an Account: Once you have chosen an exchange, you will need to create an account. This process typically involves providing your email address and creating a password. Depending on the exchange and the amount you plan to trade, you may also need to complete a Know Your Customer (KYC) process, which requires you to verify your identity and provide additional personal information.

Deposit Funds: After setting up your account, you will need to deposit funds to make a purchase. Most exchanges allow you to deposit fiat currency, such as USD or EUR, through various methods like bank transfer, credit card, or debit card. Some exchanges may also require you to deposit cryptocurrency, like Bitcoin or Ethereum, which can then be traded for XRP.

Buy XRP: With funds in your exchange account, you can now buy XRP. Navigate to the trading platform or order page and select the trading pair you wish to use (e.g., XRP/USD, XRP/BTC). Enter the amount of XRP you want to buy and execute your order. Once the order is filled, the XRP will be credited to your exchange account.

Store XRP Safely: Storing your XRP securely is crucial to protect your investment. While keeping XRP on an exchange might be convenient for trading, it may not be the safest option, as exchanges can be vulnerable to hacks or other security breaches. Instead, consider using a dedicated cryptocurrency wallet to store your XRP. There are two main types of wallets:

Software Wallets: These are applications or programs that you can download to your computer or mobile device. Software wallets, like Exodus or Atomic Wallet, offer a user-friendly interface and basic security features. However, they can still be vulnerable to malware or hacks.

Hardware Wallets: These are physical devices that securely store your private keys offline, providing a higher level of security. Hardware wallets, like Ledger Nano S or Trezor, are considered the safest way to store cryptocurrencies, including XRP. While they come with a cost, they are an excellent investment for long-term holders.

Investing in XRP involves choosing a cryptocurrency exchange, creating an account, depositing funds, buying XRP, and securely storing it in a dedicated wallet. By following these steps, you can successfully invest in XRP and protect your digital assets.

5.2 Market Performance and Price Analysis

Understanding the market performance and price analysis of XRP is crucial for both potential investors and those who already hold the digital asset. In this section, we will discuss the factors that influence XRP's price and provide a general overview of its historical market performance.

Market Dynamics: Like other cryptocurrencies, XRP's price is influenced by market dynamics such as supply and demand. The more people buy and use XRP, the higher its demand, which can potentially drive up its price. Conversely, if there is a large supply of XRP in the market or a decrease in demand, the price may drop.

Market Sentiment: The overall sentiment in the cryptocurrency market can also have a significant impact on XRP's price. Positive news, such as partnerships, new use cases, or regulatory clarity, can improve investor sentiment and lead to an increase in demand and price. On the other hand, negative news or market downturns can lead to a decrease in demand and lower prices.

Utility and Adoption: As XRP gains more real-world use cases and wider adoption, its utility increases, which can have a positive effect on its price. The more institutions and individuals that use XRP for cross-border payments, liquidity provisioning, or other applications, the higher its potential value.

Regulatory Environment: The regulatory environment surrounding cryptocurrencies can have a direct impact on XRP's price. Regulatory clarity or positive developments, such as clear guidelines or favorable legislation, can boost investor confidence and lead to increased demand. On the contrary, regulatory uncertainty or negative developments can result in decreased demand and lower prices.

Market Competition: The competition within the cryptocurrency market can also influence XRP's price. As new cryptocurrencies and blockchain projects emerge, they may compete with XRP for market share and adoption. The success of these competing projects can impact XRP's market performance and price.

Historical Performance: XRP's historical price performance can provide insights into its market trends and potential future performance. While past performance is not a guarantee of future results, it can be useful for understanding the asset's volatility and identifying patterns or trends.

XRP's market performance and price analysis are influenced by a variety of factors, including market dynamics, sentiment, utility, adoption, regulatory environment, competition, and historical performance. By considering these factors, investors can gain a better understanding of XRP's market behavior and make more informed decisions when investing in the digital asset. Keep in mind that cryptocurrency markets are notoriously volatile, and it is essential to conduct thorough research and consider your risk tolerance before making any investment decisions.

5.3 Risks and Challenges for XRP Investors

Investing in XRP, like any other investment, comes with its risks and challenges. In this section, we will discuss some of the primary risks and challenges that XRP investors may face, ensuring that you have a well-rounded understanding before making any investment decisions.

Market Volatility: Cryptocurrency markets, including XRP, are known for their high volatility. Prices can experience significant fluctuations within short periods, leading to potential gains or losses. Investors should be prepared for this volatility and consider their risk tolerance before investing in XRP.

Regulatory Uncertainty: The regulatory landscape for cryptocurrencies is still evolving, and XRP has faced its share of regulatory challenges. Changes in regulations or unfavorable rulings can have a negative impact on XRP's price and adoption, posing a risk to investors.

Security Risks: Safeguarding your XRP investment requires vigilance against potential security threats. Cyber-attacks, phishing scams, and exchange hacks are some of the risks that investors must be aware of and take necessary precautions to mitigate, such as using secure wallets and practicing good digital hygiene.

Competition: The cryptocurrency market is constantly evolving, with new projects and technologies emerging regularly. XRP faces competition from other digital assets and payment solutions that could potentially impact its adoption, utility, and market position, which in turn may affect its price.

Technological Risks: Like any technology, the XRP Ledger and RippleNet could face potential technical issues or vulnerabilities that may affect their functionality or security. While Ripple has a strong track record of maintaining and improving its technology, investors should be aware of the inherent risks associated with any technological platform.

Liquidity Risk: Although XRP is one of the top cryptocurrencies in terms of market capitalization, there may be instances where liquidity is limited, making it challenging to buy or sell XRP at desired prices. This risk is generally lower for more prominent cryptocurrencies like XRP but should still be considered by investors.

Long-term Viability: The long-term success of XRP as an investment depends on factors such as widespread adoption, regulatory clarity, and technological advancements. While XRP has demonstrated significant growth and utility, the future is uncertain, and investors should be prepared for potential challenges that could impact its long-term viability.

Investing in XRP comes with various risks and challenges, including market volatility, regulatory uncertainty, security risks, competition, technological risks, liquidity risk, and questions about long-term viability. It is crucial for investors to understand these risks, conduct thorough research, and consider their risk tolerance before committing to an investment in XRP or any other cryptocurrency.

5.4 Regulatory Framework and Compliance

The regulatory framework and compliance landscape surrounding cryptocurrencies, including XRP, play a crucial role in shaping their development, adoption, and potential success. In this section, we will discuss the current regulatory framework and compliance issues related to XRP.

Global Regulatory Landscape: Cryptocurrency regulations vary significantly across different jurisdictions. Some countries have adopted a more open and supportive stance, while others have implemented strict regulations or outright bans. Investors should be aware of the regulations in their jurisdiction and ensure that they are in compliance when investing in or using XRP.

Regulatory Bodies: Various regulatory bodies oversee the cryptocurrency market and its participants, such as the Financial Crimes Enforcement Network (FinCEN), the Securities and Exchange Commission (SEC), and the Commodity Futures Trading Commission (CFTC) in the United States. These bodies are responsible for creating and enforcing regulations that aim to protect investors, maintain market integrity, and prevent illegal activities.

Anti-Money Laundering (AML) and Know Your Customer (KYC) Regulations: Financial institutions and cryptocurrency exchanges are subject to AML and KYC regulations that aim to prevent money laundering, terrorist financing, and other illicit activities. These regulations require institutions to verify the identities of their customers and monitor transactions to detect and report suspicious activities.

Security, Currency, or Commodity: One of the significant regulatory challenges faced by XRP and other cryptocurrencies is their classification as a security, currency, or commodity. The classification determines the regulatory requirements and oversight. In the case of XRP, the SEC in the United States has claimed that XRP is an unregistered security, leading to ongoing litigation between Ripple Labs and the SEC. The outcome of this case could have significant implications for XRP's future and its regulatory treatment.

Tax Implications: Investors should be aware of the tax implications of investing in and using XRP. Depending on the jurisdiction, gains or losses from trading XRP might be subject to capital gains tax, and using XRP for purchases may also have tax consequences. It is essential to consult with a tax professional to ensure compliance with tax laws and regulations.

The regulatory framework and compliance landscape for XRP are complex and ever-evolving. Investors should be aware of the regulations in their jurisdiction, the role of regulatory bodies, AML and KYC requirements, classification challenges, and tax implications when investing in or using XRP. Staying informed about the latest regulatory developments and ensuring compliance can help mitigate potential risks and contribute to the long-term success of your investment.

Chapter 6: The Future of XRP and Ripple

6.1 XRP's Role in the Internet of Value (IoV)

The Internet of Value (IoV) is a concept that envisions a world where value, such as money or other assets, can be exchanged as easily and quickly as information is shared over the internet today. In this section, we will discuss XRP's role in the development and realization of the Internet of Value.

Frictionless Transactions: One of the key goals of the IoV is to enable frictionless transactions, allowing for near-instantaneous and low-cost transfers of value across borders. XRP's fast settlement times and minimal transaction fees make it an ideal candidate for facilitating such transactions. By offering a seamless and efficient means for value transfer, XRP can play a significant role in the IoV's development.

Interoperability: Another crucial aspect of the IoV is interoperability between different payment systems, networks, and currencies. RippleNet, the global payment network powered by Ripple's technology, aims to connect banks, payment providers, and other financial institutions, making it easier to transact using various currencies, including XRP. This interoperability helps create a more inclusive and accessible global financial system, further supporting the IoV's vision.

Liquidity Provision: Liquidity is a critical component of the IoV, as it allows for smooth and efficient value transfers. XRP can act as a bridge currency, providing on-demand liquidity for cross-border transactions and reducing the need for pre-funded nostro and vostro accounts. This role not only lowers the costs associated with traditional correspondent banking but also improves the overall efficiency of the global financial system.

Micropayments and Web Monetization: The IoV envisions a world where even the smallest transactions can be conducted quickly and cost-effectively. XRP's low fees and fast settlement times make it well-suited for micropayments and web monetization use cases, such as paying for content or services on a per-use basis or enabling direct creator-to-consumer payments. By facilitating micropayments, XRP can help unlock new economic models and opportunities on the internet.

Decentralized Finance (DeFi): The IoV also encompasses the idea of decentralized finance, which aims to provide financial services without relying on traditional intermediaries like banks. XRP can play a role in the DeFi ecosystem by enabling fast, low-cost transactions, providing liquidity, and serving as collateral for decentralized lending and borrowing platforms.

XRP has the potential to play a significant role in the Internet of Value by enabling frictionless transactions, promoting interoperability, providing liquidity, facilitating micropayments, and contributing to the DeFi ecosystem. As the IoV continues to develop and gain traction, XRP's utility and adoption could increase, further solidifying its position within the global financial system.

6.2 Central Bank Digital Currencies (CBDCs) and XRP

Central Bank Digital Currencies (CBDCs) are digital forms of fiat money issued by central banks, representing a new type of currency that could reshape the global financial system. In this section, we will discuss the relationship between CBDCs and XRP, and how XRP might interact with or support the growth of CBDCs.

Interoperability: As more countries develop and launch their CBDCs, there will be a need for seamless interactions between these digital currencies and existing financial systems. XRP, with its inherent ability to bridge different currencies, could play a significant role in facilitating interoperability between CBDCs and other digital assets, ensuring smooth cross-border transactions.

Liquidity Provision: CBDCs will require liquidity management to ensure their effective use in cross-border transactions. XRP, as a digital asset with fast settlement times and low transaction fees, can provide on-demand liquidity for CBDCs, much like it does for fiat currencies today. This ability can help reduce the costs and complexities associated with traditional correspondent banking.

CBDC Exchange: XRP can act as a bridge currency, allowing for efficient and low-cost exchange between different CBDCs. By connecting various CBDCs, XRP can facilitate cross-border transactions and global trade, making it easier for countries to transact with one another and fostering economic growth.

Enhancing CBDC Capabilities: XRP's underlying technology, the XRP Ledger, can potentially be used by central banks to develop or enhance their CBDC platforms. The XRP Ledger's consensus algorithm, transaction speed, and low fees can provide central banks with a robust and scalable infrastructure for their digital currencies, ensuring a high level of performance and security.

Impact on XRP Adoption: The rise of CBDCs could indirectly impact the adoption and utility of XRP. As more countries and central banks embrace digital currencies, the overall acceptance of digital assets, including XRP, may increase. Additionally, if XRP can successfully serve as a bridge currency and provide liquidity for CBDCs, its demand and utility could grow, further supporting its role within the global financial system.

The emergence of CBDCs presents both opportunities and challenges for XRP. By facilitating interoperability, providing liquidity, and enabling efficient exchange between CBDCs, XRP can potentially play a vital role in the growth and development of CBDCs. As the global financial landscape continues to evolve, XRP's ability to adapt and support new forms of digital currencies, such as CBDCs, will be crucial to its long-term success and relevance.

6.3 Smart Contracts and the Flare Network

Smart contracts and the Flare Network are essential components of the broader XRP ecosystem that can unlock new use cases and functionalities for XRP. In this section, we will discuss smart contracts and the Flare Network, and how they relate to XRP.

Smart Contracts: Smart contracts are self-executing contracts with the terms of the agreement directly written into code. They automatically execute when predefined conditions are met, eliminating the need for intermediaries and reducing costs, delays, and potential disputes. Smart contracts enable the creation of decentralized applications (dApps) and can revolutionize industries like finance, supply chain management, and real estate, among others.

Flare Network: The Flare Network is a decentralized network that brings smart contract functionality to the XRP Ledger. While the XRP Ledger is primarily designed for fast and low-cost payments, it does not natively support smart contracts. The Flare Network aims to address this limitation by providing a scalable and secure platform for creating and executing smart contracts using XRP.

Integration with XRP: The Flare Network integrates with the XRP Ledger through a unique consensus mechanism called the Federated Byzantine Agreement (FBA). This integration allows XRP holders to participate in the Flare Network by creating FXRP, a 1:1 representation of XRP on the Flare Network. Users can easily move their XRP between the XRP Ledger and the Flare Network, enabling them to use XRP within smart contracts and dApps on Flare.

Use Cases: By integrating smart contract functionality with the XRP Ledger, the Flare Network opens up new use cases and possibilities for XRP. Some potential use cases include decentralized finance (DeFi) applications like lending, borrowing, and staking, tokenization of real-world assets, supply chain management solutions, and more. These new use cases can further enhance the utility and adoption of XRP.

Spark Token (FLR): The Flare Network has its native token, called Spark (FLR), which is used for various purposes, such as paying for transaction fees, participating in the network's governance, and providing collateral for creating FXRP. XRP holders were eligible for a Spark token airdrop, giving them an incentive to participate in and support the Flare Network.

Smart contracts and the Flare Network bring new opportunities and functionalities to the XRP ecosystem. By enabling smart contract capabilities for XRP, the Flare Network can unlock new use cases and drive further adoption, potentially strengthening XRP's position within the global financial system.

6.4 Future Use Cases: Supply Chain, Identity Verification, and Gaming

The versatile nature of XRP and its underlying technology can be applied to various industries and use cases beyond finance. In this section, we will explore some potential future use cases for XRP in supply chain management, identity verification, and gaming.

Supply Chain Management: XRP can be utilized in supply chain management to track and verify the origin, authenticity, and journey of goods through the entire supply chain. By leveraging the transparency, security, and immutability of the XRP Ledger, businesses can create a tamper-proof record of their products, ensuring compliance with regulations and increasing consumer trust. Additionally, XRP's fast and low-cost transactions can facilitate efficient and cost-effective cross-border payments for global supply chain participants.

Identity Verification: XRP could potentially be used in identity verification systems that require secure, fast, and efficient authentication. By leveraging cryptographic signatures and the XRP Ledger's decentralized nature, users could prove their identity without the need for third-party intermediaries, reducing the risk of identity theft or fraud. Such a system could be used in various sectors, including finance, healthcare, and government services, streamlining processes and enhancing security.

Gaming: The gaming industry can benefit from integrating XRP as an in-game currency or using its underlying technology for various purposes. For instance, XRP can facilitate fast and low-cost transactions for in-game purchases or player-to-player trading. Additionally, the XRP Ledger's ability to tokenize assets can enable the creation of unique in-game items with verified ownership, which can be traded or sold across different platforms. This can lead to new economic models and revenue streams for both developers and players.

The potential future use cases for XRP extend far beyond the financial sector. By leveraging its unique features and the capabilities of the XRP Ledger, XRP can find applications in supply chain management, identity verification, and gaming, among others. As the technology matures and adoption continues to grow, these and other innovative use cases could further enhance XRP's utility and value.

7.1 The Centralization Debate

One of the most prominent criticisms surrounding XRP is the debate on centralization. In this section, we will discuss the centralization debate and its implications for XRP and Ripple.

Centralization Concerns: Some critics argue that XRP is more centralized than other cryptocurrencies like Bitcoin and Ethereum. These concerns primarily stem from Ripple's role in the XRP ecosystem, as the company holds a significant portion of the total XRP supply and has significant influence over the network's development. Critics argue that this centralization contradicts the core principles of decentralization that underpin cryptocurrencies.

Ripple's XRP Holdings: Ripple holds a large portion of the total XRP supply, with a majority of it locked in escrow accounts. Ripple releases a portion of these funds each month to fund its operations, support the XRP ecosystem, and invest in strategic partnerships. While this control over the XRP supply has raised concerns about centralization, Ripple has committed to using its holdings responsibly and transparently to avoid negatively affecting the market.

Validator Nodes: The XRP Ledger relies on a network of validator nodes to reach consensus on transactions. Ripple operates a portion of these validator nodes, which has led to concerns about its influence over the network. However, the number of independent validators on the XRP Ledger has been growing over time, reducing Ripple's control and making the network more decentralized. Moreover, Ripple has no unique powers over the validators and cannot control their actions.

Ripple's Influence on Development: Ripple plays a significant role in the development and maintenance of the XRP Ledger. While this may create an impression of centralization, it's essential to note that the XRP Ledger is an open-source project, and its development is not solely controlled by Ripple. Other developers and organizations can contribute to the project, ensuring a diverse and decentralized development process.

while there are centralization concerns surrounding XRP, it is important to consider the nuances of the debate. Ripple has taken steps to increase the decentralization of the XRP Ledger and maintain transparency in its operations. As the ecosystem continues to evolve and more independent participants join the network, the centralization debate may become less of an issue for XRP and its community.

7.2 The SEC vs. Ripple: Lawsuits and Implications

In December 2020, the U.S. Securities and Exchange Commission (SEC) filed a lawsuit against Ripple Labs Inc.

and its executives, claiming that they conducted an unregistered securities offering by selling XRP. In this section, we will discuss the lawsuit and its implications for Ripple and XRP.

The SEC's Allegations: The SEC alleges that Ripple, along with its CEO, Brad Garlinghouse, and its co-founder, Chris Larsen, raised over $1.3 billion through an ongoing, unregistered securities offering of XRP since 2013. According to the SEC, XRP should be considered a security rather than a currency or commodity, and thus, its sale must comply with federal securities laws.

Ripple's Defense: Ripple has argued that XRP is not a security, but rather a digital asset used for cross-border payments and remittances. The company asserts that XRP is similar to other cryptocurrencies like Bitcoin and Ethereum, which the SEC does not classify as securities. Ripple also contends that the SEC's lawsuit is an attack on the entire cryptocurrency industry and that the regulatory agency has failed to provide clear guidance on the classification of digital assets.

Market Impact: The SEC's lawsuit has had a significant impact on XRP's market performance. Following the announcement of the lawsuit, several cryptocurrency exchanges delisted or suspended the trading of XRP, and its market value experienced a sharp decline. However, XRP has since recovered some of its value as the case proceeds and the market sentiment adjusts to the ongoing legal battle.

Implications for Ripple and XRP: The outcome of the SEC lawsuit could have far-reaching implications for Ripple, XRP, and the broader cryptocurrency ecosystem. If Ripple were to lose the case, it could face significant penalties, and XRP's classification as a security could hinder its use in the global payment ecosystem. On the other hand, if Ripple were to win the case or reach a settlement with the SEC, it could set a precedent for future regulatory actions involving digital assets and potentially strengthen XRP's position in the market.

The SEC vs. Ripple lawsuit is a pivotal event in the cryptocurrency industry, with potential implications for the future regulatory landscape of digital assets. The outcome of the case could shape XRP's future and its role in the global financial system. As the legal battle unfolds, it is crucial for investors and stakeholders to monitor the developments and understand their potential impact on XRP and the broader cryptocurrency market.

7.3 Environmental Concerns and XRP's Energy Efficiency

As the environmental impact of cryptocurrencies gains increasing attention, it is crucial to examine the energy efficiency of various digital assets. In this section, we will discuss the environmental concerns associated with cryptocurrencies and explore how XRP's energy efficiency sets it apart from other popular cryptocurrencies.

Environmental Concerns: The energy consumption of cryptocurrencies, particularly those that use Proof-of-Work

(PoW) consensus algorithms like Bitcoin, has raised significant environmental concerns. The PoW process requires massive computational power, resulting in high energy consumption and a substantial carbon footprint. As a result, the sustainability and long-term viability of PoW-based cryptocurrencies have been called into question.

XRP's Consensus Mechanism: Unlike Bitcoin and other PoW-based cryptocurrencies, XRP uses a different consensus mechanism called the Ripple Protocol Consensus Algorithm (RPCA). The RPCA does not require miners to perform complex computations to validate transactions. Instead, it relies on a network of validator nodes that reach an agreement on the validity of transactions through a voting process. This approach is considerably more energy-efficient than PoW, resulting in lower energy consumption and a reduced environmental impact.

Energy Efficiency Comparison: XRP's energy efficiency is evident when comparing its energy consumption to that of other cryptocurrencies. For example, Bitcoin's energy consumption is estimated to be around 707 kWh per transaction, while Ethereum's is approximately 62.56 kWh per transaction. In contrast, XRP's energy consumption is a mere 0.0079 kWh per transaction, making it vastly more energy-efficient and environmentally friendly.

Implications for Adoption: XRP's energy efficiency could become a significant advantage as environmental concerns continue to shape the cryptocurrency landscape. As governments, businesses, and individuals become more environmentally conscious, the demand for sustainable financial solutions may increase. XRP's low energy consumption and minimal carbon footprint could make it an attractive option for environmentally responsible investors and organizations seeking to adopt cryptocurrencies for various use cases.

The environmental concerns surrounding cryptocurrencies are a critical factor to consider in the digital asset space. XRP's energy-efficient consensus mechanism and low environmental impact set it apart from other popular cryptocurrencies, positioning it as a more sustainable alternative. As awareness of the environmental impact of cryptocurrencies grows, XRP's energy efficiency could become an increasingly important factor in its adoption and long-term success.

Chapter 8: XRP Community and Ecosystem
8.1 The Role of the XRP Community

The XRP community plays a vital role in the growth and development of the XRP ecosystem. In this section, we will explore the importance of the XRP community and how it contributes to the success and adoption of the cryptocurrency.

Grassroots Support: The XRP community is known for its passion and dedication to the project. This grassroots support helps promote the adoption and awareness of XRP and its related technologies. Community members actively engage in discussions, share news, and provide insights on social media platforms and forums, creating a robust and supportive network for XRP enthusiasts and newcomers alike.

Open-Source Development: The XRP Ledger is an open-source project, which means that its source code is freely available for anyone to review, modify, and contribute to. The XRP community plays a crucial role in the development of the XRP Ledger by providing feedback, reporting bugs, and suggesting new features. This collaborative approach ensures a diverse and decentralized development process that benefits from the expertise and knowledge of various community members.

Advocacy and Education: The XRP community actively advocates for the adoption of XRP and its underlying technologies. By organizing meetups, hosting webinars, and creating educational content, community members help educate others about the benefits and use cases of XRP. This advocacy and educational work helps expand the reach of XRP and encourages new users and businesses to consider the cryptocurrency for their financial needs.

Third-Party Projects and Applications: The XRP community has also been instrumental in building and supporting third-party projects and applications that leverage the XRP Ledger. These projects range from wallets and exchanges to decentralized applications (dApps) and platforms that use XRP for various use cases. By developing and promoting these projects, the XRP community helps expand the ecosystem and showcase the versatility of the cryptocurrency.

Feedback and Accountability: The XRP community provides valuable feedback to Ripple and other stakeholders in the ecosystem. By expressing their opinions, concerns, and suggestions, community members help ensure that the development and direction of XRP remain aligned with the needs and expectations of its users. This feedback loop helps maintain a healthy and transparent relationship between the XRP community and the organizations driving the cryptocurrency's growth.

The XRP community plays a critical role in the success and growth of the XRP ecosystem. Through grassroots support, open-source development, advocacy, education, and the creation of third-party projects, the XRP community contributes to the expansion and adoption of the cryptocurrency. As the XRP ecosystem continues to evolve, the support and involvement of the XRP community will remain essential to its long-term success.

8.2 XRP Community Initiatives and Projects

The XRP community is actively involved in various initiatives and projects that contribute to the growth and adoption of the cryptocurrency. In this section, we will discuss some of the most notable community-driven initiatives and projects within the XRP ecosystem.

XRP Tip Bot: The XRP Tip Bot is a popular community-developed application that enables users to send and receive small amounts of XRP as tips on social media platforms like Twitter, Reddit, and Discord. By facilitating micropayments, the XRP Tip Bot demonstrates the potential of XRP for instant and low-cost transactions, while also promoting community engagement and fostering a culture of generosity.

XRPL Labs: XRPL Labs is an independent development studio focused on building applications and tools for the XRP Ledger. Founded by Wietse Wind, a prominent XRP community member, XRPL Labs has developed various projects, including the XUMM wallet, which allows users to manage their XRP holdings and interact with the XRP Ledger. XRPL Labs has received funding from Ripple's Xpring initiative, highlighting the synergy between community-driven projects and Ripple's support.

Coil: Coil is a web monetization platform that uses XRP to facilitate micropayments to content creators. Founded by former Ripple CTO Stefan Thomas, Coil integrates with the Interledger Protocol (ILP) to stream XRP payments in real-time as users consume content. While Coil is not exclusively an XRP community project, its adoption and promotion by the community have contributed to its growth and success.

XRP Charities: The XRP community is also involved in various charitable initiatives, leveraging the cryptocurrency's fast and low-cost transactions for philanthropic purposes. For example, the XRP community has supported charitable campaigns like the XRP Tree Project, which aimed to plant trees in response to the carbon footprint of cryptocurrencies. These initiatives showcase the potential of XRP for social good while fostering a sense of unity and purpose within the community.

XRP Community Blog: The XRP Community Blog is a platform where community members can share their insights, opinions, and research on various aspects of XRP and the broader cryptocurrency ecosystem. By providing a space for community-generated content, the XRP Community Blog helps foster knowledge-sharing and collaboration among XRP enthusiasts.

The XRP community is actively involved in a range of initiatives and projects that contribute to the growth and adoption of the cryptocurrency. From micropayment applications like the XRP Tip Bot to development studios like XRPL Labs, these community-driven efforts showcase the versatility of XRP and help expand its reach across various use cases. As the XRP ecosystem continues to evolve, the ongoing support and innovation from the XRP community will remain crucial to its success.

8.3 XRP Developer Tools and Resources

To support the growth and adoption of XRP, a variety of developer tools and resources have been made available by Ripple and the XRP community. These resources help developers build and deploy applications on the XRP

Ledger, fostering innovation and expanding the XRP ecosystem. In this section, we will discuss some of the most popular and useful developer tools and resources available for working with XRP.

XRP Ledger Developer Portal: The XRP Ledger Developer Portal, maintained by Ripple, is the primary source of documentation, guides, and tools for developers working with the XRP Ledger. The portal provides comprehensive information on various aspects of the XRP Ledger, including its architecture, consensus algorithm, and APIs. It also offers tutorials and sample code to help developers get started with building applications on the platform.

RippleAPI: RippleAPI is the official JavaScript library for interacting with the XRP Ledger. It provides a simple and user-friendly interface for developers to submit transactions, query ledger data, and manage accounts. RippleAPI is well-documented and comes with examples to help developers integrate XRP into their applications quickly and efficiently.

XRPL.js: XRPL.js is an open-source JavaScript library developed by Ripple that enables developers to interact with the XRP Ledger using a simple and intuitive API. This library simplifies complex tasks, such as transaction signing and submission, and supports a wide range of XRP Ledger features. XRPL.js is well-maintained and continuously updated to include the latest enhancements and improvements.

XUMM SDK: The XUMM SDK is a software development kit provided by XRPL Labs that allows developers to build applications that integrate with the XUMM wallet. By leveraging the XUMM SDK, developers can create seamless and secure user experiences for managing XRP assets and interacting with the XRP Ledger.

Testnet and Faucet: Ripple provides a public testnet for developers to test their applications and experiment with the XRP Ledger without using real funds. The testnet is an exact replica of the main XRP Ledger, offering the same features and functionalities. To help developers get started, Ripple also provides a faucet service that distributes test XRP for use on the testnet.

XRP Ledger Explorer: The XRP Ledger Explorer is a valuable tool for developers and users alike, allowing them to explore and visualize transactions, accounts, and ledger data on the XRP Ledger. This tool helps developers monitor the progress of their applications and troubleshoot any issues that may arise.

A wide array of developer tools and resources are available for those looking to build applications on the XRP Ledger. These resources, combined with the active support of the XRP community, make it easy for developers to create innovative solutions that leverage the speed, scalability, and cost-efficiency of XRP. As more developers join the XRP ecosystem, the continued availability and improvement of these tools and resources will be crucial for fostering innovation and driving adoption.

The XRP community comprises a diverse group of individuals who contribute to the growth and adoption of XRP and the Ripple ecosystem. Some prominent community members and influencers have played a significant role in promoting, developing, and providing insightful commentary on XRP-related topics. In this section, we will discuss some of these key figures within the XRP community.

David Schwartz: As the Chief Technology Officer (CTO) of Ripple and one of the original architects of the XRP Ledger, David Schwartz is a highly respected figure within the XRP community. He actively engages with the community through social media, conferences, and interviews, providing valuable insights and updates on XRP and the Ripple ecosystem.

Wietse Wind: Wietse Wind is the founder of XRPL Labs, an independent development studio focused on building applications and tools for the XRP Ledger. As a prominent community member, Wind has contributed significantly to the XRP ecosystem through projects like the XUMM wallet and the XRP Tip Bot. He is also active on social media, sharing updates and engaging with the XRP community.

Hodor: Hodor is a pseudonymous XRP community member known for their insightful and well-researched blog posts on various XRP-related topics. Although Hodor is no longer active, their blog remains an essential resource for those interested in understanding the XRP ecosystem's various aspects.

Tiffany Hayden: Tiffany Hayden is a vocal XRP advocate and community member who frequently shares her thoughts and opinions on XRP and the cryptocurrency space. As a former validator operator and contributor to the XRP ecosystem, Hayden provides valuable insights and commentary on XRP-related developments.

Brad Garlinghouse: As the CEO of Ripple, Brad Garlinghouse is an influential figure in the XRP community. He often speaks at industry events and conferences, sharing Ripple's vision for XRP and the broader Internet of Value. Garlinghouse also engages with the community through social media and interviews, providing updates on Ripple's progress and addressing key concerns within the ecosystem.

Crypto Eri: Crypto Eri is a popular XRP-focused content creator on YouTube, providing news, analysis, and commentary on XRP and Ripple-related developments. Through her informative and engaging videos, Crypto Eri has become a trusted source of information for many in the XRP community.

These prominent XRP community members and influencers play a vital role in promoting, developing, and providing insightful commentary on XRP-related topics. By engaging with the community and sharing their knowledge and expertise, they contribute to the growth and adoption of XRP and the Ripple ecosystem. As the XRP landscape continues to evolve, the ongoing involvement of these key figures will remain crucial in shaping its future direction and success.

Chapter 9: XRP-Compatible Wallets and Exchanges
9.1 Types of XRP Wallets: Hardware, Software, and Paper

To store and manage XRP, users need a compatible wallet. There are several types of XRP wallets available, each with its own advantages and disadvantages. In this section, we will discuss the three primary types of XRP wallets: hardware, software, and paper wallets.

Hardware Wallets: Hardware wallets are physical devices designed to store private keys securely offline. These wallets offer the highest level of security, as they are immune to online hacking attempts and malware. To access and manage their XRP, users connect the hardware wallet to a computer or mobile device. Some popular hardware wallets that support XRP include Ledger Nano S, Ledger Nano X, and Trezor Model T. While hardware wallets provide excellent security, they can be more expensive than other wallet options.

Software Wallets: Software wallets are applications that users can install on their computers or mobile devices. They store private keys digitally and allow users to manage their XRP easily. Software wallets come in various forms, such as desktop wallets, mobile wallets, and browser extensions. Examples of XRP-compatible software wallets include XUMM, Exodus, and Atomic Wallet. While software wallets offer convenience and ease of use, they may be more vulnerable to hacking and malware than hardware wallets.

Paper Wallets: Paper wallets are physical printouts of a user's private keys and XRP public address. They are created using a paper wallet generator, which ensures the private key is never exposed to an internet-connected device. Users store the printout in a safe place and access their XRP by importing the private key into a software or hardware wallet when needed. Paper wallets offer a high level of security, as they are not susceptible to online hacking. However, they can be less convenient to use and may be prone to physical damage or loss.

Hardware, software, and paper wallets each offer unique benefits and drawbacks for storing and managing XRP. Users should consider their security requirements, convenience, and budget when choosing the right wallet option. It is also essential to research and select reputable wallet providers to ensure the safekeeping of XRP assets.

9.2 How to Choose the Right XRP Wallet

Choosing the right XRP wallet is crucial for the secure storage and management of your XRP assets. The ideal wallet will depend on your individual needs and preferences. Here are some key factors to consider when selecting the right XRP wallet:

Security: The primary concern when choosing a wallet should be its security features. Hardware wallets are considered the most secure, as they store private keys offline and are immune to online hacking attempts. Software wallets provide a good balance between security and convenience but can be more susceptible to malware and hacking. Paper wallets offer robust security, but you must ensure they are stored safely and protected from physical damage or loss. Always opt for a wallet with a strong reputation for security.

Convenience: Consider how often you will need to access and manage your XRP assets. If you require quick and easy access, a software wallet may be more suitable, as they are readily available on your computer or mobile device. Hardware wallets provide secure storage but may be less convenient due to the need to connect them to a device. Paper wallets can be secure but are the least convenient for regular use.

User Interface: A user-friendly interface is essential, especially for those new to cryptocurrencies. Look for a wallet that is easy to navigate and understand, with clear instructions and a well-designed layout. This will make managing your XRP more enjoyable and less confusing.

Backup and Recovery: Ensure that the wallet you choose has a reliable backup and recovery system in place. This will help you regain access to your XRP if your wallet is lost, damaged, or compromised. Hardware and software wallets typically provide a recovery phrase or seed words during setup, which you must store securely. For paper wallets, keep multiple copies in different secure locations.

Compatibility: Ensure the wallet is compatible with your preferred devices, such as computers, smartphones, or tablets. Some wallets are designed specifically for certain operating systems or platforms, so choose one that aligns with your needs.

Customer Support: Opt for a wallet provider with a strong track record of customer support. This can be helpful if you ever encounter issues or have questions about using the wallet.

Community Reputation: Research the wallet's reputation within the XRP community. Check user reviews, ratings, and feedback to gauge the overall sentiment and satisfaction with the wallet.

By considering these factors, you can make a well-informed decision when selecting the right XRP wallet to meet your needs. Remember to prioritize security and choose a wallet from a reputable provider to ensure the safekeeping of your XRP assets.

9.3 Popular XRP Wallets: Features and Security

There are several popular XRP wallets available, each with its own set of features and security measures. Here, we will discuss some of the most well-known wallets, their features, and the security they provide.

Ledger Nano S/X: The Ledger Nano S and Ledger Nano X are hardware wallets known for their top-notch security features. These wallets store your private keys offline and protect them with a secure element chip. They support multiple cryptocurrencies, including XRP, and are compatible with various wallet software, such as Ledger Live. The Ledger Nano X also offers Bluetooth connectivity for added convenience. Both wallets require a PIN code to access, and users receive a recovery phrase during setup for backup and recovery purposes.

Trezor Model T: Trezor Model T is another hardware wallet that supports XRP and numerous other cryptocurrencies. It features a touchscreen interface for ease of use and stores private keys offline, ensuring maximum security. Like Ledger wallets, Trezor Model T requires a PIN code for access and provides a recovery phrase for backup and recovery.

XUMM: XUMM is a software wallet designed specifically for XRP. It is available for both Android and iOS devices and focuses on simplicity and user-friendliness. XUMM offers a range of features, including support for multiple XRP accounts, QR code scanning for transactions, and transaction signing for advanced users. Security-wise, XUMM encrypts private keys on the device, and users must create a PIN code to access the wallet.

Exodus: Exodus is a desktop and mobile software wallet that supports XRP and over 100 other cryptocurrencies. It boasts an intuitive user interface and offers features like built-in exchange functionality and portfolio tracking. Exodus stores private keys locally on your device and encrypts them for added security. The wallet also provides a backup and recovery system using a 12-word recovery phrase.

Atomic Wallet: Atomic Wallet is a software wallet available for desktop and mobile platforms, supporting XRP and over 300 other cryptocurrencies. It features a built-in exchange, staking options, and atomic swaps for decentralized trading. Atomic Wallet secures private keys on your device and provides a 12-word recovery phrase for backup and recovery.

When choosing an XRP wallet, it is crucial to select one that aligns with your security requirements, convenience preferences, and device compatibility. Always opt for reputable wallets with a proven track record and robust security features to protect your XRP assets.

9.4 XRP on Cryptocurrency Exchanges: A Comprehensive Guide

Cryptocurrency exchanges play a vital role in the XRP ecosystem, allowing users to buy, sell, and trade XRP for other cryptocurrencies or fiat currencies. This guide will provide a comprehensive overview of XRP on cryptocurrency exchanges, with a focus on factors to consider when choosing an exchange, popular exchanges for XRP trading, and the process of buying and selling XRP on exchanges.

Factors to consider when choosing an exchange:

Reputation: Select an exchange with a good reputation within the cryptocurrency community. Check reviews, user feedback, and news about the exchange to gauge its credibility.

Security: Opt for an exchange with strong security measures, including two-factor authentication (2FA), cold storage for funds, and regular security audits.

Fees: Exchanges charge various fees, including trading fees, deposit fees, and withdrawal fees. Compare these fees among different exchanges to find the most cost-effective option.

Supported currencies: Ensure the exchange supports the cryptocurrencies or fiat currencies you want to trade with XRP.

Trading volume and liquidity: High trading volume and liquidity can help facilitate smooth and efficient trading, as well as provide better price stability.

User interface and support: Look for an exchange with an easy-to-use interface and responsive customer support to assist with any issues or questions.

Popular exchanges for XRP trading:

Several well-known exchanges support XRP trading, including:

Binance: Binance is a leading cryptocurrency exchange with a wide selection of cryptocurrencies and trading pairs. It offers XRP trading against multiple cryptocurrencies and stablecoins.

Coinbase: Coinbase is a popular exchange known for its user-friendly platform and support for fiat currency trading. Users can buy, sell, and trade XRP against USD, EUR, and other fiat currencies on Coinbase.

Kraken: Kraken is a reputable exchange that supports XRP trading against various cryptocurrencies and fiat currencies, such as USD, EUR, and GBP.

Bitstamp: Bitstamp is a long-established exchange that offers XRP trading against multiple cryptocurrencies and fiat currencies, including USD and EUR.

Buying and selling XRP on exchanges:

Create an account: To get started, create an account on your chosen exchange. This typically involves providing your email address, creating a password, and verifying your identity.

Deposit funds: Deposit the cryptocurrency or fiat currency you wish to trade for XRP. This can be done through bank transfers, credit/debit cards, or other supported payment methods.

Place an order: Once your funds are available, place a buy order for XRP. There are different types of orders, such as market orders (executed immediately at the current market price) and limit orders (executed only when the desired price is reached). Choose the order type that best suits your needs.

Store your XRP: After buying XRP, you can either store it on the exchange or transfer it to a personal wallet for added security. Remember that storing your assets on an exchange can expose them to potential hacking risks.

Selling XRP: To sell XRP, deposit it into your exchange account, and place a sell order. Once the order is executed, you can withdraw the funds to your bank account or transfer them to another cryptocurrency wallet.

By considering the factors mentioned above and following the steps outlined, you can confidently navigate the world of XRP trading on cryptocurrency exchanges.

Chapter 10: Taxation and Legal Compliance for XRP
10.1 Understanding Cryptocurrency Taxes

Cryptocurrency taxes can be complex, but it's essential to understand the basics to ensure legal compliance. Here, we will provide a general overview of cryptocurrency taxes and how they may apply to XRP. Please note that tax regulations vary between jurisdictions, and it's crucial to consult with a tax professional in your country for specific guidance.

Taxable events: In many countries, specific events related to cryptocurrencies are considered taxable. These events typically include:

Selling cryptocurrencies for fiat currency (e.g., selling XRP for USD)

Trading one cryptocurrency for another (e.g., exchanging XRP for Bitcoin)

Using cryptocurrencies to purchase goods or services (e.g., using XRP to buy a product)

Mining or receiving cryptocurrencies as income (e.g., earning XRP through a job or as rewards)

Capital gains and losses: When you sell or trade cryptocurrencies, you may incur capital gains or losses. Capital gains occur when the value of the cryptocurrency has increased since you acquired it, while capital losses occur when the value has decreased. The difference between the cost basis (the original price paid for the cryptocurrency) and the sale price determines your capital gain or loss.

In many jurisdictions, short-term capital gains (assets held for less than a year) are taxed at a higher rate than long-term capital gains (assets held for more than a year).

Recordkeeping: To accurately calculate your capital gains or losses and ensure tax compliance, it's essential to keep detailed records of your cryptocurrency transactions. This includes information such as:

The date of the transaction

The value of the cryptocurrency in your local currency at the time of the transaction

The cost basis of the cryptocurrency

Any fees or expenses associated with the transaction

Tax reporting: You may be required to report your cryptocurrency transactions on your annual tax return. This usually involves completing specific tax forms, calculating your total capital gains or losses, and including this information with your tax filing.

Tax planning: To minimize your tax liability, you can consider strategies such as:

Holding your cryptocurrencies for more than a year to qualify for lower long-term capital gains tax rates

Using tax-loss harvesting to offset capital gains with capital losses

Ensuring accurate and up-to-date recordkeeping to avoid underreporting or overreporting your gains and losses

Understanding the basic principles of cryptocurrency taxes and how they apply to XRP is crucial for legal compliance. Always consult with a tax professional in your jurisdiction for personalized advice and guidance on your specific tax situation.

10.2 Tax Implications for XRP Holders

As an XRP holder, you need to be aware of the tax implications associated with owning and transacting with XRP. Here, we will provide a general overview of the tax implications for XRP holders. Remember that tax regulations can vary by jurisdiction, so it's essential to consult a tax professional in your country for specific guidance.

Capital gains and losses: Just like with other cryptocurrencies, when you sell, trade, or use XRP to make purchases, you may incur capital gains or losses. These are calculated based on the difference between the cost basis (the original price you paid for the XRP) and the sale price. Depending on the holding period, you may be subject to short-term or long-term capital gains tax rates.

Income tax: If you receive XRP as payment for goods or services, or as rewards from mining, staking, or participating in liquidity pools, this income may be subject to income tax. The taxable amount is generally calculated based on the fair market value of XRP at the time you receive it.

Airdrops and forks: In some jurisdictions, receiving XRP through airdrops or forks may be considered a taxable event. The tax implications can vary depending on the specific circumstances and the regulations in your country.

Gifts and donations: If you gift XRP to someone, you may not be subject to capital gains tax, but the recipient may be liable for taxes if they later sell or trade the XRP. In some jurisdictions, donating XRP to a qualified charitable organization may provide tax benefits, such as a deduction from your taxable income.

Inheritance and estate tax: Inheriting XRP may also have tax implications, depending on the jurisdiction. There may be inheritance or estate taxes applied to the inherited XRP, and the new owner may be subject to capital gains tax when they eventually sell or trade the XRP.

Tax reporting and recordkeeping: As an XRP holder, it's essential to keep accurate records of your transactions, including dates, values, and cost basis. This information is necessary for calculating your capital gains or losses and reporting them on your tax return.

To ensure you comply with tax regulations in your jurisdiction, consult a tax professional who can provide guidance specific to your situation. Being aware of the tax implications of holding and transacting with XRP will help you make informed decisions and avoid potential issues with tax authorities.

10.3 International Taxation and Regulatory Considerations

International taxation and regulatory considerations play a crucial role in cryptocurrency investments, including XRP. As the regulatory landscape evolves, it's essential for XRP holders to be aware of these factors. Here, we provide a general overview of international taxation and regulatory considerations for XRP holders. Always consult a tax professional in your country for personalized guidance.

Cross-border transactions: If you engage in cross-border transactions with XRP, such as sending or receiving XRP from individuals or entities in other countries, you need to be aware of the tax regulations in both the sending and receiving jurisdictions. The tax implications may vary depending on the specific regulations in each country.

Tax residency and dual-residency: Your tax residency status can impact your tax obligations related to XRP. Most countries tax their residents on their worldwide income, which includes income derived from cryptocurrency transactions. If you are a resident of more than one country or have changed your tax residency, you may be subject to tax obligations in multiple jurisdictions.

Foreign asset reporting: In some countries, you may be required to report your foreign-held cryptocurrency assets, including XRP, if they exceed a certain threshold. This reporting may be separate from your regular income tax filing and could require you to provide detailed information about your XRP holdings and transactions.

Tax treaties: Some countries have tax treaties in place to prevent double taxation and facilitate tax information exchange between countries. These treaties may impact your tax obligations related to XRP, particularly if you are a resident of one treaty country and hold XRP in another treaty country.

Regulatory compliance: In addition to tax considerations, you need to be aware of the regulatory requirements related to XRP in the countries where you hold, transact, or engage in other activities with XRP. Regulatory requirements can include anti-money laundering (AML) and know-your-customer (KYC) obligations, as well as licensing requirements for certain activities, such as operating an exchange or offering XRP-based financial products.

Ongoing regulatory developments: The regulatory landscape for cryptocurrencies, including XRP, is continually evolving. It's crucial to stay informed about regulatory changes in your jurisdiction and any countries where you engage in XRP transactions. This will help you ensure ongoing compliance and avoid potential legal issues.

International taxation and regulatory considerations are essential aspects of owning and transacting with XRP. By staying informed and seeking guidance from tax professionals, you can navigate these complexities and ensure compliance with the relevant regulations in your jurisdiction and globally.

10.4 Best Practices for Tax Reporting and Compliance

To ensure proper tax reporting and compliance when dealing with XRP and other cryptocurrencies, it's important to follow a set of best practices. Here, we outline some general best practices to help you stay compliant with tax regulations and avoid potential issues with tax authorities.

Maintain accurate records: Keep thorough records of all your XRP transactions, including the date, amount, and the value of the transaction in your local currency. This information will be crucial when calculating capital gains or losses and reporting them on your tax return.

Determine your cost basis: Your cost basis is the original value of the XRP when you acquired it, and it's used to calculate your capital gains or losses. Make sure to track the cost basis for each XRP transaction to accurately report your gains or losses.

Track holding periods: The length of time you hold XRP can impact the tax rate applied to your capital gains or losses. Keep track of your holding periods to determine if your gains or losses are short-term or long-term, which may be subject to different tax rates.

Stay informed about tax laws: Tax laws related to cryptocurrencies, including XRP, can change frequently. Stay updated on the latest regulations in your jurisdiction to ensure you're aware of any changes that might affect your tax obligations.

Use tax software or a tax professional: Managing cryptocurrency taxes can be complicated, and errors can lead to issues with tax authorities. Consider using specialized tax software or consulting a tax professional with experience in cryptocurrency taxation to ensure accurate reporting and compliance.

Report all taxable events: Don't overlook any taxable events related to your XRP holdings. This includes not only selling or trading XRP but also using it for purchases, receiving it as payment, and participating in airdrops, forks, staking, or mining.

Be aware of international tax considerations: If you engage in cross-border transactions or hold XRP in foreign accounts, be aware of the tax implications and reporting requirements in the relevant jurisdictions.

Understand your local tax authority's guidance: Familiarize yourself with any guidance provided by your local tax authority related to cryptocurrency taxation. This will help you ensure compliance with the specific rules and requirements in your jurisdiction.

Keep a backup of your records: Maintain a secure backup of all your XRP transaction records and tax-related documents. In case of an audit or a need to amend a previous tax return, having this information readily available will be invaluable.

By following these best practices, you can minimize the risk of tax-related issues and ensure that you're accurately reporting your XRP-related income and transactions. As always, consult a tax professional for personalized guidance based on your specific situation and jurisdiction.

Chapter 11: Privacy and Security in the XRP Ecosystem

11.1 Privacy Features of XRP Transactions

Privacy is an important aspect of any financial transaction, and XRP is no exception. Although XRP transactions are transparent and recorded on a public ledger, there are certain privacy features in place to protect users' identities and maintain a level of privacy.

Pseudonymous addresses: Like most cryptocurrencies, XRP uses pseudonymous addresses to represent users on the network. These addresses, which are strings of alphanumeric characters, serve as public identifiers for transactions without directly revealing the user's personal information. However, it's worth noting that sophisticated analysis techniques may still link addresses to individuals in some cases.

No IP address tracking: XRP transactions do not directly include the IP address of the sender or recipient. This helps to protect users' privacy by not revealing their location or internet service provider.

Destination tags: XRP employs a feature called "destination tags," which allows users to include an additional identifier with their transactions. Destination tags are especially useful when sending XRP to an exchange or other service that uses a single XRP address for multiple users. By including a unique destination tag, users can maintain privacy by not revealing their specific account or user ID.

Transaction memos: XRP transactions allow users to include an optional "memo" field, which can contain an encrypted message or other information. This feature can help maintain privacy by allowing users to communicate or share sensitive information without revealing it on the public ledger.

However, it's essential to understand that XRP transactions are not entirely private, as the ledger records all transactions, and the transaction history of any address can be publicly viewed. Additionally, exchanges and other services may require users to provide personal information for regulatory compliance purposes, which could potentially link users' identities to their XRP addresses.

While XRP offers some privacy features, it should not be considered a fully anonymous or privacy-focused cryptocurrency. Users looking for a higher level of privacy may want to explore other cryptocurrencies specifically designed for privacy, such as Monero or Zcash.

11.2 Security Best Practices for XRP Holders

Securing your XRP holdings is crucial to prevent potential losses due to hacking, phishing, or other malicious activities. Here are some security best practices that XRP holders should follow to safeguard their investments:

Use a secure wallet: Choose a reputable and secure wallet to store your XRP. Hardware wallets, such as Ledger or Trezor, are considered the most secure options, as they store your private keys offline and protect them from online threats.

Keep your private keys safe: Never share your private keys with anyone, as they give full access to your XRP holdings. Store your private keys offline in a secure location, such as a safety deposit box, or use a hardware wallet to keep them protected.

Enable two-factor authentication (2FA): Whenever possible, enable 2FA on your wallet, exchange accounts, or any other platform where you store or manage your XRP. This adds an extra layer of security by requiring a second form of authentication, such as a one-time code from an authenticator app or a hardware security key.

Use strong, unique passwords: Create strong and unique passwords for all your accounts, including wallets and exchanges. Avoid using the same password for multiple accounts, as this makes it easier for attackers to gain access to your funds.

Regularly update software: Keep your wallet software, operating system, and any other applications you use to manage your XRP up to date. Regular updates help to protect against known security vulnerabilities.

Be cautious with links and emails: Always double-check the URLs of websites you visit, and never click on suspicious links or download email attachments from unknown sources. Phishing attacks, where attackers impersonate legitimate services to steal your login information, are a common threat in the cryptocurrency space.

Monitor your accounts: Regularly review your XRP transactions and account activity to detect any unauthorized access or suspicious activity. Set up notifications, if available, to alert you of any unusual transactions or login attempts.

Don't disclose your holdings: Avoid discussing your XRP holdings, especially on public forums or social media. Revealing your investments can make you a target for hackers or scammers.

Be wary of scams and too-good-to-be-true offers: Cryptocurrency markets are sometimes targeted by scammers offering unrealistic returns or posing as support staff. Always verify the legitimacy of any offers, and never send your XRP to an unknown address without proper research.

By following these security best practices, you can significantly reduce the risk of losing your XRP to cyberattacks or other malicious activities. It's essential to remain vigilant and prioritize the security of your digital assets to enjoy the benefits of the XRP ecosystem safely.

11.3 Protecting Against Hacks, Scams, and Phishing Attacks

In the world of cryptocurrencies, protecting your assets from hacks, scams, and phishing attacks is of utmost importance. Here are some essential tips to help you stay safe and secure:

Verify website URLs: Before entering any sensitive information or logging into a website, always double-check the URL to ensure it is legitimate. Look for the padlock symbol in the address bar, which indicates a secure connection. Scammers often create fake websites with similar URLs to trick users into revealing their login credentials.

Be cautious with emails and messages: Be wary of unexpected emails or messages from unknown sources, especially those containing links or attachments. Always verify the sender's identity before clicking on any links or downloading any files. Avoid responding to messages asking for personal or financial information.

Use two-factor authentication (2FA): Enable 2FA on all your accounts, including wallets and exchanges. This adds an additional layer of security by requiring a second form of authentication, such as a one-time code from an authenticator app or a hardware security key.

Do not share sensitive information: Never share your private keys, passwords, or other sensitive information with anyone, even if they claim to be from a reputable organization. Legitimate companies will never ask for your private keys or passwords.

Research before investing: Always research projects, platforms, or services before investing your XRP. Check for reviews, read whitepapers, and verify the legitimacy of the company or team behind the project. Be cautious of offers that promise high returns or seem too good to be true.

Keep software up-to-date: Regularly update your wallet software, operating system, and any other applications you use to manage your XRP. This helps protect against known security vulnerabilities.

Use strong, unique passwords: Create strong and unique passwords for all your accounts, including wallets and exchanges. Avoid using the same password for multiple accounts, as this makes it easier for attackers to gain access to your funds.

Monitor your accounts: Regularly review your XRP transactions and account activity to detect any unauthorized access or suspicious activity. Set up notifications, if available, to alert you of any unusual transactions or login attempts.

Educate yourself: Stay informed about the latest security threats, scams, and best practices in the cryptocurrency space. The more knowledgeable you are, the better equipped you will be to protect yourself and your assets.

By following these guidelines, you can significantly reduce the risk of falling victim to hacks, scams, and phishing attacks. Being cautious and vigilant in the ever-evolving world of cryptocurrencies will help you enjoy the benefits of the XRP ecosystem securely and confidently.

11.4 The Importance of Personal Data Protection

In the digital age, personal data protection has become increasingly important, especially in the world of cryptocurrencies. Protecting your personal information is crucial for several reasons:

Identity theft prevention: Cybercriminals can use your personal data, such as your name, address, and social security number, to commit identity theft. They can apply for loans, credit cards, or even file taxes in your name, causing serious financial and legal problems.

Financial security: By protecting your personal data, you can prevent unauthorized access to your bank accounts, cryptocurrency wallets, and other financial assets. This helps to keep your hard-earned money safe from fraudsters and hackers.

Reputation management: Sensitive personal information, if leaked or mishandled, can damage your reputation or expose you to blackmail and other forms of harassment. Ensuring that your data is secure helps maintain your privacy and personal integrity.

Compliance with regulations: Various jurisdictions have data protection laws in place, such as the General Data Protection Regulation (GDPR) in the European Union. These regulations require individuals and businesses to take appropriate measures to safeguard personal data, and non-compliance can result in hefty fines and legal penalties.

Trust and credibility: In the cryptocurrency space, trust is paramount. Protecting your personal data demonstrates to others that you take security and privacy seriously, fostering trust and credibility within the community.

To protect your personal data in the XRP ecosystem and beyond, consider the following measures:

Limit the amount of personal information you share online, especially on social media and public forums.

Be cautious when providing your data to third parties, and ensure they have a legitimate reason and proper security measures in place.

Use strong and unique passwords for all your accounts and enable two-factor authentication wherever possible.

Keep your devices secure by installing the latest updates and using reputable antivirus software.

Be mindful of phishing attempts and verify the legitimacy of websites, emails, and messages before clicking on links or providing any sensitive information.

By prioritizing personal data protection, you can navigate the world of cryptocurrencies and the XRP ecosystem with greater confidence, security, and peace of mind.

Chapter 12: XRP in the Broader Cryptocurrency Landscape
12.1 Comparing XRP to Bitcoin, Ethereum, and Other
Cryptocurrencies

XRP stands out in the cryptocurrency market for its unique characteristics and use cases. To better understand XRP's position within the broader landscape, let's compare it to some of the other leading cryptocurrencies, such as Bitcoin and Ethereum.

Speed and Scalability: One of the most significant differences between XRP and other cryptocurrencies is its transaction speed and scalability. XRP transactions are processed in just 3-5 seconds, compared to Bitcoin's 10-minute average confirmation time and Ethereum's 15-30 seconds. XRP can handle up to 1,500 transactions per second, while Bitcoin can only process around 7 transactions per second, and Ethereum can handle around 30. This makes XRP highly efficient for cross-border transactions and other use cases that require quick transaction times and high throughput.

Energy Consumption: XRP is considerably more energy-efficient than both Bitcoin and Ethereum. This is because XRP uses a consensus mechanism called the Ripple Protocol Consensus Algorithm (RPCA) to validate transactions, which consumes significantly less energy than the Proof of Work (PoW) mining systems employed by Bitcoin and Ethereum. As a result, XRP is often considered a more sustainable and environmentally friendly cryptocurrency option.

Use Cases: While Bitcoin is primarily seen as a store of value and digital gold, and Ethereum is known for its smart contracts and decentralized applications (dApps), XRP is mainly used for cross-border payments, remittances, and liquidity provisioning. RippleNet, the global payment network built on the XRP Ledger, enables banks and financial institutions to execute fast and cost-effective transactions using XRP as a bridge currency.

Decentralization: The decentralization of cryptocurrencies is a crucial factor for many investors and users. Bitcoin and Ethereum are often considered more decentralized than XRP, mainly because Ripple, the company behind XRP, holds a large portion of the total XRP supply. However, Ripple has taken steps to address these concerns by placing a significant amount of XRP in escrow and working to increase the number of independent validators on the XRP Ledger.

Market Capitalization: In terms of market capitalization, XRP often ranks within the top 10 cryptocurrencies, although it trails behind both Bitcoin and Ethereum. Market capitalization represents the total value of a cryptocurrency, calculated by multiplying the current price by the total circulating supply. While XRP has experienced significant growth and adoption, it has not yet reached the same level of prominence as Bitcoin or Ethereum.

XRP has distinct advantages and use cases compared to other cryptocurrencies like Bitcoin and Ethereum. Its speed, scalability, and energy efficiency make it an attractive option for cross-border payments and other specific applications. However, it's essential to consider factors such as decentralization and market capitalization when evaluating XRP in the broader cryptocurrency landscape.

12.2 Interoperability with Other Blockchains and Networks

Interoperability refers to the ability of different blockchain networks and systems to communicate and work together seamlessly. This feature is essential in the cryptocurrency space as it enables diverse platforms to interact and exchange information, enhancing the overall functionality and utility of the entire ecosystem. In the context of XRP, interoperability plays a crucial role in enabling the cryptocurrency to fulfill its mission of revolutionizing cross-border payments and other use cases.

Interledger Protocol (ILP): One of the primary tools that facilitate XRP's interoperability is the Interledger Protocol (ILP). ILP is an open-source protocol developed by Ripple that allows for secure and efficient transfers between different ledgers and payment systems. By using ILP, XRP can easily connect with other blockchains and traditional financial networks, enabling seamless transactions across various platforms. This feature is particularly valuable for cross-border payments, where users need to transfer funds between different currencies and payment systems.

Atomic Swaps: Atomic swaps are another technology that enhances XRP's interoperability with other cryptocurrencies. Atomic swaps enable the direct, trustless exchange of cryptocurrencies between users on different blockchains without the need for a third party, such as a cryptocurrency exchange. These swaps utilize smart contract technology to ensure that both parties receive their respective assets simultaneously, reducing the risk of fraud or loss. Although XRP does not natively support smart contracts, it can still participate in atomic swaps through platforms like the Flare Network or other third-party solutions.

Wrapping XRP: Wrapped tokens are another way to achieve interoperability between XRP and other blockchain networks, particularly those based on Ethereum. By "wrapping" XRP into an ERC-20 token, it becomes compatible with the Ethereum network and its vast ecosystem of decentralized applications (dApps) and smart contracts. This enables XRP holders to access various DeFi services, such as lending, borrowing, and yield farming, directly from their XRP holdings without converting to another cryptocurrency.

Integration with Decentralized Finance (DeFi) Platforms: As the DeFi sector continues to grow, more platforms are integrating XRP to expand their user base and offer additional services. XRP's fast transaction times and low fees make it an attractive option for DeFi platforms, enhancing its interoperability with other cryptocurrencies and blockchain networks. Examples of DeFi platforms that support XRP include Flare Network, Kava, and Forte, among others.

XRP's interoperability with other blockchains and networks is crucial for its success in revolutionizing cross-border payments and other use cases. Technologies like the Interledger Protocol, atomic swaps, wrapped tokens, and integration with DeFi platforms enable XRP to interact seamlessly with various networks, providing users with a diverse range of services and capabilities.

12.3 The Role of Stablecoins and XRP's Place in the Stablecoin Ecosystem

Stablecoins are a type of cryptocurrency designed to minimize price fluctuations by pegging their value to a stable asset, such as a fiat currency (e.g., US dollars) or a commodity like gold. They play an essential role in the cryptocurrency landscape by providing a stable store of value, reducing volatility risks, and facilitating seamless transactions between different digital assets.

The Function of Stablecoins in the Crypto Ecosystem: Stablecoins serve various purposes in the cryptocurrency landscape, including:

Reducing Volatility: By maintaining a stable value, stablecoins help mitigate the risks associated with the volatile nature of cryptocurrencies, making them a popular choice for traders and investors looking to hedge against market fluctuations.

Enabling Seamless Transactions: Stablecoins can be easily exchanged with other cryptocurrencies, making them a convenient option for cross-currency transactions, remittances, and payments.

Providing Access to Decentralized Finance (DeFi) Services: With their stable value, stablecoins have become a popular choice in the DeFi space, allowing users to access various financial services such as lending, borrowing, and yield farming without worrying about price volatility.

XRP's Place in the Stablecoin Ecosystem: Although XRP is not a stablecoin itself, it plays a significant role in the stablecoin ecosystem by facilitating transactions and interactions between stablecoins and other cryptocurrencies. Some ways XRP contributes to the stablecoin ecosystem include:

Interledger Protocol (ILP): As mentioned earlier, ILP enables seamless transactions between different blockchains and payment systems. This feature is particularly valuable for stablecoin transactions, allowing users to easily exchange various stablecoins across multiple platforms.

Bridge Currency: XRP can serve as a bridge currency for cross-currency transactions involving stablecoins. By using XRP as an intermediary, users can exchange one stablecoin for another quickly and efficiently, without the need for multiple conversions.

Integration with DeFi Platforms: As more DeFi platforms integrate XRP, it becomes easier for XRP holders to interact with various stablecoins within these platforms. This integration allows users to access DeFi services using XRP, while also benefiting from the stability offered by stablecoins.

While XRP is not a stablecoin, it plays a crucial role in the stablecoin ecosystem by facilitating transactions and interactions between stablecoins and other cryptocurrencies. By leveraging its unique features, such as the Interledger Protocol and its potential as a bridge currency, XRP helps enhance the functionality and utility of stablecoins within the broader cryptocurrency landscape.

12.4   The Impact of Decentralized Finance (DeFi) on XRP

Decentralized Finance, or DeFi, refers to a suite of financial services built on blockchain technology that aims to provide a more accessible, open, and efficient alternative to traditional financial systems. These services include lending, borrowing, trading, and earning interest on digital assets, among others. DeFi has experienced tremendous growth in recent years, and its impact on XRP and the Ripple ecosystem is significant.

XRP in DeFi Lending and Borrowing Platforms: DeFi lending and borrowing platforms enable users to lend their digital assets to earn interest or borrow assets against collateral. The integration of XRP in these platforms allows XRP holders to participate in DeFi lending and borrowing activities, thereby unlocking new ways to earn passive income and access liquidity.

XRP in Decentralized Exchanges (DEXs): Decentralized exchanges facilitate peer-to-peer trading of digital assets without relying on a central authority. By being listed on DEXs, XRP becomes more accessible to users, increasing its liquidity and trading volume. Additionally, XRP can be used as a base currency for trading pairs, making it easier for users to exchange between various digital assets.

XRP and DeFi Yield Farming: Yield farming is a popular DeFi practice where users "farm" digital assets to earn rewards, typically in the form of tokens. When XRP is integrated into DeFi yield farming platforms, XRP holders can stake or provide liquidity to earn additional rewards, giving them more opportunities to grow their digital asset portfolio.

XRP and DeFi Interoperability: DeFi platforms often operate on different blockchains, which can make it challenging for users to move assets between platforms. As XRP is designed for cross-chain interoperability, it can serve as a bridge asset between different DeFi platforms, simplifying transactions and increasing the efficiency of the DeFi ecosystem.

Flare Network and XRP: The Flare Network is a blockchain protocol designed to bring smart contract functionality to the XRP ecosystem, enabling XRP holders to access a wide range of DeFi services. With the integration of the Flare Network, XRP holders can participate in DeFi activities like staking, lending, and yield farming using XRP-backed assets, expanding the use cases of XRP within the DeFi space.

The growth of DeFi has had a substantial impact on XRP and the Ripple ecosystem. By integrating with DeFi platforms and services, XRP becomes a more versatile digital asset, enabling its holders to participate in various DeFi activities, access new income streams, and benefit from the broader DeFi ecosystem. This integration not only strengthens XRP's position in the cryptocurrency market but also contributes to the ongoing growth and evolution of the DeFi space.

Chapter 13: Case Studies of XRP Adoption

13.1 Financial Institutions Embracing XRP

The adoption of XRP by financial institutions has been growing steadily due to its ability to facilitate faster, cheaper, and more efficient cross-border transactions. In this section, we will explore some notable case studies of financial institutions that have embraced XRP and the positive impact it has had on their operations.

Santander Bank: Santander, one of the largest banks in the world, has been an early adopter of XRP and Ripple's technology. They launched a mobile app called One Pay FX, which uses Ripple's xCurrent technology to enable fast, secure, and low-cost international money transfers. By incorporating XRP into their payment infrastructure, Santander has managed to reduce transaction costs and improve the overall customer experience.

SBI Remit and Siam Commercial Bank (SCB): SBI Remit, a leading remittance service provider in Japan, partnered with Siam Commercial Bank (SCB) in Thailand to leverage Ripple's technology and XRP for cross-border transactions between the two countries. This partnership has enabled faster and more affordable remittance services for customers, greatly improving the efficiency of cross-border payments between Japan and Thailand.

MoneyGram: MoneyGram, a global money transfer company, partnered with Ripple in 2019 to use the digital asset XRP for cross-border transactions. The partnership allowed MoneyGram to leverage the XRP Ledger's fast and low-cost transaction capabilities, resulting in significant cost savings and improved transaction speeds. However, it should be noted that this partnership was suspended in 2021 due to the ongoing SEC lawsuit against Ripple. Despite the suspension, the initial success of this partnership demonstrated the potential benefits of using XRP for remittance services.

American Express and LianLian Pay: American Express has collaborated with Ripple to streamline cross-border transactions using Ripple's blockchain technology. This partnership has enabled American Express to provide faster and more transparent payment services to its customers. In addition, American Express partnered with LianLian Pay, a Chinese payment provider, which also uses Ripple's technology, to further enhance payment services between the US and China.

Standard Chartered Bank: Standard Chartered Bank, a multinational banking and financial services company, has been working with Ripple to improve its cross-border payment services. By incorporating Ripple's technology and XRP, Standard Chartered has managed to reduce transaction costs and processing times, resulting in a better experience for its customers.

These case studies showcase the growing adoption of XRP by financial institutions worldwide. By leveraging XRP and Ripple's technology, these organizations have managed to improve the efficiency of their cross-border payment services, reduce costs, and provide a better experience for their customers. As more financial institutions continue to recognize the potential benefits of XRP and its underlying technology, its adoption is expected to grow further, solidifying its position in the global financial ecosystem.

13.2 XRP in Emerging Markets: Remittance and Financial Inclusion

XRP has shown great potential in emerging markets, particularly in the areas of remittance and financial inclusion. In this section, we will explore how XRP is being utilized to address the challenges faced by these markets and improve the lives of millions of people.

Remittance:

Remittance is a significant source of income for many people in emerging markets, especially those with family members working abroad. Traditional remittance methods, such as banks and money transfer operators, can be slow, expensive, and unreliable. XRP offers a promising alternative by providing fast, low-cost, and secure transactions that are well-suited for remittance services.

Several companies and initiatives have recognized the potential of XRP for remittance services in emerging markets. For instance, the partnership between SBI Remit and Siam Commercial Bank, as mentioned earlier, has improved remittance services between Japan and Thailand. Similarly, other remittance companies, such as SendFriend, FlashFX, and Mercury FX, have also adopted XRP to facilitate affordable and efficient cross-border transactions for their customers.

Financial Inclusion:

Financial inclusion is a pressing issue in emerging markets, where millions of people lack access to formal banking services. This limits their ability to save, invest, and access credit, resulting in a lower quality of life and reduced economic growth.

XRP and its underlying technology can play a crucial role in promoting financial inclusion in emerging markets. By leveraging XRP's fast, low-cost transactions and decentralized nature, innovative solutions can be developed to provide unbanked and underbanked individuals with access to essential financial services.

For example, mobile money services, which have gained significant popularity in regions such as Africa, can be enhanced using XRP to facilitate instant and cost-effective transactions. This can help expand the reach of mobile money services, further promoting financial inclusion.

XRP can also be used to facilitate microloans and other forms of credit for people in emerging markets, enabling them to invest in businesses, education, and other opportunities that can help improve their lives and contribute to economic growth.

XRP's unique features, such as its speed, low transaction costs, and decentralized nature, make it well-suited for addressing the challenges faced by emerging markets. By facilitating more efficient remittance services and promoting financial inclusion, XRP has the potential to transform the lives of millions of people and contribute to the development of these markets.

13.3 Examples of Successful XRP Integration in Business Operations

In this section, we will explore some examples of businesses that have successfully integrated XRP into their operations, illustrating the various benefits and efficiencies that can be achieved by embracing this innovative technology.

Coil:

Coil is a web monetization platform that enables content creators to receive payments for their work through micropayments. By integrating XRP into its payment system, Coil allows creators to be paid in real-time as users consume their content, without the need for traditional subscription models or paywalls. This not only provides a more seamless experience for users but also allows content creators to access a more diverse and global audience.

Bitso:

Bitso is a leading cryptocurrency exchange in Latin America that has integrated XRP as a key component of its cross-border payment service. By using XRP as a bridge currency, Bitso is able to offer its customers faster and more cost-effective international money transfers. This has been particularly beneficial for remittance flows between the United States and Mexico, where Bitso has seen significant growth in transaction volume.

Nexo:

Nexo is a digital asset lending platform that allows users to obtain instant loans backed by their cryptocurrency holdings, including XRP. By accepting XRP as collateral, Nexo has expanded its customer base and enabled XRP holders to access credit without having to sell their digital assets. This not only provides a valuable financial service for XRP users but also contributes to increased liquidity in the XRP market.

Omni:

Omni was a sharing-economy platform (acquired by Coinbase in 2019) that allowed users to rent and share various items, such as bikes, tools, and storage space. The platform integrated XRP as a payment option, enabling users to earn XRP for renting out their possessions. This integration not only showcased the versatility of XRP as a payment method but also helped to introduce cryptocurrency to a broader audience.

These examples illustrate the diverse ways in which XRP can be integrated into various business operations, providing tangible benefits such as cost savings, increased efficiency, and expanded market reach. As more businesses begin to recognize the potential of XRP and its underlying technology, it is likely that we will see even more innovative and transformative use cases in the coming years.

13.4 Lessons Learned from XRP Implementations

In this section, we will analyze the lessons learned from various XRP implementations across different industries and how these insights can guide future endeavors to make the most out of the XRP ecosystem.

Importance of Collaboration:

Successful XRP implementations often involve close collaboration between stakeholders, such as financial institutions, businesses, regulators, and developers.

Establishing strong partnerships and fostering open communication channels can lead to better integration and smoother adoption of XRP-based solutions, as well as address any concerns or challenges that may arise during implementation.

Tailoring Solutions to Specific Needs:

XRP-based solutions should be customized to address the unique requirements and pain points of the target industry or market. By focusing on the specific needs of a particular sector, XRP implementers can create more effective and targeted solutions that bring about meaningful improvements in efficiency, cost savings, and user experience.

User-Friendly Interfaces:

To encourage widespread adoption of XRP-based solutions, it is crucial to develop user-friendly interfaces that are easy to understand and navigate, even for non-technical users. Simplifying the user experience can help break down barriers to entry and make it more accessible to a broader audience, ultimately driving greater adoption and acceptance of XRP.

Regulatory Compliance:

Navigating the regulatory landscape is a key consideration for any XRP implementation, as it can have a significant impact on the success and viability of the project. By proactively engaging with regulators and ensuring compliance with applicable laws and regulations, businesses can mitigate potential legal risks and build trust with their customers and partners.

Ongoing Education and Support:

Educating users and partners about the benefits of XRP and providing ongoing support is essential for successful implementations. By actively addressing misconceptions, promoting awareness, and offering technical assistance, businesses can help drive the adoption of XRP-based solutions and ensure their long-term success.

Iterative Approach:

Implementing XRP solutions is often an iterative process, involving continuous improvement, learning, and adaptation. By monitoring user feedback, assessing performance metrics, and staying up-to-date with developments in the XRP ecosystem, businesses can refine their implementations and make necessary adjustments to better serve their customers and partners.

In summary, the lessons learned from XRP implementations highlight the importance of collaboration, customization, user-friendliness, regulatory compliance, education, and iterative improvement. By taking these factors into account, businesses can successfully integrate XRP into their operations and unlock the full potential of this innovative digital asset.

14.1 XRP and Financial Inclusion: Empowering the Unbanked

Financial inclusion refers to the accessibility and availability of financial services to all individuals, regardless of their income or social status. This concept is particularly important for the unbanked population, which consists of individuals who do not have access to traditional banking services. XRP has the potential to play a significant role in promoting financial inclusion and empowering the unbanked through various initiatives and use cases.

Low-Cost Remittances:

One of the main challenges faced by the unbanked population is the high cost of sending money across borders, which can take a significant portion of their income. XRP enables fast and cost-effective cross-border transactions, making remittance services more accessible and affordable for those who rely on them. By lowering the fees associated with international money transfers, XRP can help improve the financial well-being of millions of people who depend on remittances to support themselves and their families.

Access to Basic Financial Services:

XRP, through its integration with various financial platforms, can help the unbanked population gain access to basic financial services such as savings, loans, and insurance. By leveraging the power of XRP, these platforms can provide low-cost, accessible financial products tailored to the needs of the unbanked population. This increased access to financial services can help lift people out of poverty and promote economic growth in underprivileged communities.

Mobile Money Solutions:

With the proliferation of mobile phones, even in remote and underprivileged areas, mobile money solutions have emerged as a powerful tool to promote financial inclusion. XRP can be integrated into mobile money platforms, enabling users to make transactions, pay bills, and access various financial services directly from their mobile devices. By tapping into the ubiquity of mobile phones, XRP-based solutions can reach a wider audience and provide much-needed financial services to those who have been historically underserved.

Microfinance:

Microfinance institutions (MFIs) provide small loans and other financial services to low-income individuals and entrepreneurs who are unable to access traditional banking services. XRP can facilitate the operations of MFIs by lowering transaction costs, improving efficiency, and enabling real-time settlement. By leveraging XRP, MFIs can serve more clients and provide better financial products, thus contributing to economic development and financial inclusion.

Digital Identity:

A lack of proper identification can be a significant barrier to accessing financial services for the unbanked population. XRP, combined with blockchain technology, can help create decentralized digital identity systems that securely store and verify personal information, making it easier for the unbanked to access financial services. By providing a secure, verifiable digital identity, XRP-based solutions can help bridge the gap between the unbanked and the world of finance.

XRP has the potential to empower the unbanked population by providing low-cost remittances, facilitating access to basic financial services, enabling mobile money solutions, supporting microfinance institutions, and offering digital identity solutions. By promoting financial inclusion, XRP can help drive socioeconomic development and improve the lives of millions of people around the world.

14.2 The Role of XRP in Reducing Remittance Costs

Remittances are funds sent by migrant workers back to their home countries, often to support their families. These transactions are crucial for many economies, particularly in developing countries. However, traditional remittance channels, such as banks and money transfer operators, often charge high fees, making it expensive for people to send money across borders. XRP can play a vital role in reducing remittance costs, making it more affordable for individuals to send money home.

Speed:

Traditional remittance services can take several days to process cross-border transactions. This slow process often results in higher fees for the sender, as intermediaries charge additional costs for holding and transferring the funds. XRP transactions, on the other hand, can be settled in just a few seconds, significantly reducing the time and costs associated with cross-border transfers.

Low Transaction Fees:

XRP boasts minimal transaction fees, often costing just fractions of a cent per transaction. This is in stark contrast to the fees charged by banks and money transfer operators, which can range from 3% to 10% of the transaction amount. By utilizing XRP for remittances, individuals can save a substantial amount of money in fees, allowing them to send more funds to their loved ones.

Currency Exchange:

One of the primary reasons remittance costs are high is the need to convert currencies. When transferring money across borders, the sender's currency must be converted into the recipient's currency, often involving multiple intermediaries and currency conversions. Each conversion incurs a fee, which adds up quickly. XRP can act as a bridge currency, allowing for direct conversions between different currencies without the need for multiple intermediaries. This process reduces the overall cost of currency conversion, making remittance transactions more affordable.

Decentralization:

XRP operates on a decentralized ledger, which means that transactions are not controlled by any single entity, such as a bank or government. This decentralization can help lower remittance costs by eliminating the need for intermediaries who charge fees for their services. By cutting out the middlemen, XRP can facilitate more direct, affordable money transfers between parties.

Scalability:

The XRP Ledger is designed to handle a high volume of transactions, making it well-suited for remittance services. As the demand for remittance transactions grows, the XRP Ledger can scale accordingly without sacrificing speed or affordability. This scalability ensures that XRP can continue to provide cost-effective remittance solutions as the global remittance market expands.

XRP can significantly reduce remittance costs by offering faster transaction speeds, lower fees, more efficient currency exchange, decentralization, and scalability. By making it more affordable for individuals to send money across borders, XRP has the potential to positively impact the lives of millions of people who rely on remittances to support themselves and their families.

14.3 XRP and Environmental Sustainability: A Greener Cryptocurrency

Cryptocurrencies have faced criticism for their impact on the environment, particularly those that use Proof of Work (PoW) consensus mechanisms, such as Bitcoin. PoW requires significant energy consumption as miners compete to solve complex mathematical problems, which in turn leads to a substantial carbon footprint. XRP, however, uses a different consensus mechanism called the Ripple Protocol Consensus Algorithm (RPCA), making it a more environmentally friendly cryptocurrency option.

Energy-Efficient Consensus Mechanism:

The RPCA, unlike PoW, does not rely on energy-intensive mining processes. Instead, it uses a network of validators that reach consensus on the state of the ledger, without the need for competition or extensive computational power. This consensus mechanism consumes significantly less energy, making XRP more sustainable and reducing its impact on the environment.

Lower Carbon Footprint:

As a result of its energy-efficient consensus mechanism, XRP has a much smaller carbon footprint compared to other cryptocurrencies. By choosing XRP over more energy-intensive options, users can contribute to a greener and more sustainable cryptocurrency ecosystem. This is particularly important as concerns about climate change and environmental damage continue to grow.

Scalability and Sustainability:

The XRP Ledger is designed to handle a high volume of transactions with minimal energy consumption, making it a scalable and sustainable solution for various financial applications, including remittances, cross-border payments, and decentralized finance. As the demand for digital financial services continues to increase, XRP's energy-efficient design allows it to grow and adapt without exacerbating environmental concerns.

Ripple's Environmental Initiatives:

Ripple, the company behind XRP, is also committed to environmental sustainability. In 2020, Ripple announced its goal to become carbon neutral by 2030. The company is working to reduce its carbon emissions and invest in sustainable technology and carbon removal projects. Additionally, Ripple has partnered with organizations like the Energy Web Foundation to decarbonize public blockchains and drive the broader adoption of renewable energy sources within the cryptocurrency industry.

XRP stands out as a greener cryptocurrency option due to its energy-efficient consensus mechanism, lower carbon footprint, scalability, and Ripple's commitment to environmental sustainability. By choosing XRP, users can contribute to a more sustainable future for both the cryptocurrency sector and the planet.

14.4 The Future of Work and XRP's Impact on the Global Economy

The future of work is rapidly changing, driven by advancements in technology and the increasing globalization of the economy. As more people participate in the digital economy, cryptocurrencies like XRP can play a crucial role in shaping the global financial landscape. Here are some ways XRP could impact the future of work and the global economy:

Cross-Border Payments and Freelancers:

As remote work becomes more prevalent, freelancers and independent contractors are taking on projects from clients around the world. XRP can facilitate faster, cheaper, and more efficient cross-border payments, enabling freelancers to receive their earnings without the delays and high fees associated with traditional banking systems. This can lead to more financial opportunities and greater income stability for workers in the global gig economy.

Financial Inclusion and Micro-Entrepreneurship:

Many individuals in developing countries lack access to traditional banking services, which can limit their ability to participate in the global economy. XRP can help bridge this gap by providing a means for unbanked individuals to access financial services, opening up new opportunities for micro-entrepreneurship and small business growth. By leveraging XRP for transactions and remittances, these individuals can create new income streams and contribute to the overall economic growth of their communities.

Accelerating the Adoption of Digital Currencies:

As XRP continues to gain traction, it may encourage the wider adoption of digital currencies for everyday transactions. This can help to diversify the global economy, reduce reliance on centralized financial institutions, and promote economic resilience in the face of potential crises. Additionally, XRP's energy-efficient design could encourage the development of more sustainable cryptocurrencies, contributing to a greener financial ecosystem.

Facilitating Trade and Investment:

XRP's ability to quickly and efficiently process transactions could have a significant impact on international trade and investment. By reducing the time and cost associated with cross-border payments, XRP can help businesses access new markets, streamline supply chains, and foster economic growth. This increased connectivity could lead to a more integrated and prosperous global economy.

XRP has the potential to significantly impact the future of work and the global economy by facilitating cross-border payments, promoting financial inclusion, accelerating the adoption of digital currencies, and fostering international trade and investment. As the digital economy continues to evolve, XRP's role in shaping the financial landscape is likely to grow, creating new opportunities for individuals and businesses alike.

Chapter 15: XRP as a Potential Reserve Currency

15.1 The Concept of Reserve Currencies: A Brief Overview

A reserve currency is a foreign currency that is held in significant quantities by governments and institutions as part of their foreign exchange reserves. These reserves are used to facilitate international trade, finance, and investments. Reserve currencies play a crucial role in the global economy and are typically characterized by their stability, liquidity, and widespread acceptance.

Traditionally, reserve currencies have been the domain of major world economies, with the US Dollar, Euro, Japanese Yen, and British Pound being the most prominent examples. These currencies are often used as a reference for determining the value of other currencies and can act as a safe haven during times of economic uncertainty.

The concept of a reserve currency has several key features:

Stability: Reserve currencies are usually backed by stable and powerful economies. This stability is important because it provides confidence to governments and institutions holding the currency as part of their reserves. In times of economic turmoil, a stable reserve currency can serve as a safe haven, protecting against currency fluctuations and devaluation.

Liquidity: A reserve currency must be easily convertible into other currencies and widely accepted in international trade. High liquidity is essential because it allows governments and institutions to quickly access funds in the reserve currency when needed, without causing significant market disruptions or price fluctuations.

Widespread Acceptance: Reserve currencies are accepted as a means of payment in international transactions, making it easier for countries to trade and invest with one another. This widespread acceptance also helps promote global economic integration and growth.

As the world becomes more connected and digital, the idea of cryptocurrencies like XRP serving as a reserve currency has gained traction. Proponents argue that digital currencies, with their borderless nature, fast transaction times, and low fees, could offer a more efficient alternative to traditional reserve currencies. However, for XRP or any other cryptocurrency to become a reserve currency, it would need to demonstrate stability, liquidity, and widespread acceptance on a global scale.

15.2 Key Factors for Reserve Currency Status

For a currency to be considered as a reserve currency, there are several key factors that need to be met:

Economic Strength: The currency must be backed by a strong economy, as this provides confidence in its long-term stability. A country with a large and robust economy can better support the value of its currency, making it more attractive for other nations to hold as a reserve currency.

Political Stability: Political stability is important because it reduces the risk of sudden policy changes that could negatively impact the value of the currency. A stable political environment also provides a more predictable framework for international trade and investment.

Trust and Confidence: A reserve currency should inspire trust and confidence in its value and stability. This can be achieved through strong institutions, sound monetary policy, and a track record of maintaining its value over time.

Wide Acceptance and Convertibility: A reserve currency must be easily convertible into other currencies and widely accepted for international trade and investment. This helps facilitate global economic transactions and reduces the need for countries to hold multiple currencies in their reserves.

Network Effect: The more countries and institutions that adopt a currency as a reserve, the more likely it is to be widely accepted and maintain its status as a reserve currency. This network effect can create a self-reinforcing cycle, where increased adoption leads to further trust and confidence in the currency.

Low Inflation and Interest Rates: A reserve currency should maintain low inflation and interest rates to preserve its purchasing power and attractiveness as a store of value. High inflation or interest rates can erode the value of the currency and make it less desirable as a reserve.

For XRP or any other cryptocurrency to achieve reserve currency status, it would need to meet these key factors. While XRP has certain advantages, such as fast transaction times and low fees, it currently falls short in areas like economic strength and political stability, as it is not backed by a central government or economy. Additionally, the widespread acceptance and network effect required for reserve currency status have not yet been achieved for XRP or any other cryptocurrency. Nonetheless, as the digital economy continues to evolve, cryptocurrencies may be able to overcome these challenges and play a more significant role in the global financial system.

While XRP has not yet achieved reserve currency status, it does possess several strengths that make it a compelling candidate for this role:

Speed: XRP transactions are extremely fast, often settling in just 3-5 seconds. This is a significant improvement over traditional currencies, which can take hours or even days for international transactions to clear. Speed is crucial in a global economy where rapid transactions are increasingly important.

Low Transaction Costs: XRP boasts minimal transaction fees, making it more cost-effective for international transfers and currency exchanges. Reduced transaction costs can lead to increased efficiency in global trade and make XRP an attractive option for countries looking to diversify their reserve holdings.

Scalability: XRP is designed to handle a large volume of transactions, with the ability to process up to 1,500 transactions per second. This scalability is essential for a reserve currency, as it needs to be able to handle a high volume of transactions without suffering from congestion or delays.

Environmental Sustainability: Unlike cryptocurrencies like Bitcoin, which rely on energy-intensive mining processes, XRP uses a consensus algorithm that requires significantly less energy. This makes XRP a more environmentally friendly option, which could be a factor that attracts nations concerned about the environmental impact of their reserve holdings.

Decentralization: Although there is an ongoing debate about the level of decentralization in the XRP ecosystem, its decentralized nature could be appealing for countries seeking a reserve currency that is less subject to the control of a single government or central bank.

Interoperability: XRP is designed to be interoperable with various blockchain networks and traditional financial systems. This flexibility allows XRP to act as a bridge between different currencies, making it an attractive option for facilitating global trade and investment.

Despite these strengths, it's important to note that XRP faces several challenges in becoming a reserve currency, including gaining widespread acceptance, achieving economic and political stability, and overcoming regulatory hurdles. However, as the global financial landscape continues to evolve, XRP's strengths could potentially play a role in shaping the future of reserve currencies.

15.3.1 Speed, Scalability, and Cost Efficiency

Speed, scalability, and cost efficiency are key features of XRP that make it stand out among other cryptocurrencies and traditional financial systems. Here's a simple explanation of these three factors:

Speed: In the context of cryptocurrencies, speed refers to how quickly transactions can be processed and confirmed. XRP's transactions are known for their speed, often settling in just 3-5 seconds. This is much faster than other popular cryptocurrencies like Bitcoin, which can take anywhere from 10 minutes to an hour or more to confirm transactions, and traditional financial systems, which may take days for international transactions to clear. Speed is essential for a global economy that demands rapid, real-time transactions.

Scalability: Scalability means the ability of a system to handle a growing number of transactions without suffering from delays or performance issues. XRP is highly scalable, with the capacity to process up to 1,500 transactions per second. This level of scalability is crucial for a cryptocurrency to be widely adopted and used in various financial applications, as it ensures that the system can handle high transaction volumes without becoming congested or slow.

Cost Efficiency: Cost efficiency refers to the affordability of conducting transactions on a particular network. XRP has very low transaction fees, typically costing fractions of a penny per transaction. This is significantly cheaper than many other cryptocurrencies and traditional financial systems, which can charge high fees for international transfers and currency exchanges. Low transaction costs make XRP an attractive option for individuals and businesses looking to save money on fees, as well as for countries considering the adoption of XRP for various financial applications.

XRP's speed, scalability, and cost efficiency make it a compelling option for various financial use cases, including cross-border payments, remittances, and potentially even as a reserve currency. Its ability to process transactions quickly, handle high volumes of transactions, and offer affordable fees sets it apart from other cryptocurrencies and traditional financial systems.

15.3.2 Decentralization and Security

Decentralization and security are two important factors that contribute to XRP's potential as a reserve currency. Here's a simple explanation of these concepts:

Decentralization: Decentralization means that a system is not controlled by a single entity or organization. Instead, control and decision-making are distributed across a network of participants. In the case of XRP, the XRP Ledger is maintained by a network of validators that come to a consensus on the state of the ledger. This makes the system more resistant to censorship, manipulation, and single points of failure. Decentralization is considered a key feature of cryptocurrencies, as it promotes fairness and prevents any one party from having too much control over the network.

Security: Security refers to the measures in place to protect a system from attacks, fraud, and other malicious activities. In the context of XRP, security is achieved through the use of cryptography, which ensures that transactions are secure and cannot be tampered with. The XRP Ledger also employs a consensus protocol that requires validators to agree on the state of the ledger, making it difficult for any single participant to manipulate the system. Additionally, the network is constantly monitored for unusual activity, and suspicious transactions can be flagged and investigated.

Decentralization and security are crucial aspects of XRP that make it a viable candidate for a reserve currency. Its decentralized nature ensures that no single entity has too much control over the network, promoting fairness and stability. Meanwhile, strong security measures protect the integrity of transactions and keep the system safe from malicious actors. These features contribute to the overall trustworthiness of XRP, making it an attractive option for various financial applications and as a potential reserve currency.

15.3.3 Network Effects and Global Acceptance

Network effects and global acceptance are two more factors that contribute to XRP's potential as a reserve currency. Let's break down these concepts in simple terms:

Network Effects: Network effects occur when a product or service becomes more valuable as more people use it. In the context of cryptocurrencies like XRP, as more people and institutions adopt the currency for transactions and hold it as an asset, its value and utility increase. This creates a positive feedback loop: as the network grows, it attracts even more users, further increasing the value and utility of the currency. For XRP to become a viable reserve currency, it must continue to grow its user base and strengthen its network effects.

Global Acceptance: Global acceptance refers to the widespread adoption and recognition of a currency around the world. A currency that is globally accepted can be easily exchanged for goods, services, or other currencies, making it more useful and reliable as a store of value and medium of exchange. In the case of XRP, its global acceptance is growing as more financial institutions, businesses, and individuals start using it for cross-border payments, remittances, and other financial transactions. As XRP gains recognition and acceptance worldwide, its potential to serve as a reserve currency increases.

Network effects and global acceptance are important factors that contribute to XRP's potential as a reserve currency. As the network continues to grow and attract more users, its value and utility increase. Meanwhile, greater global acceptance means that XRP is more likely to be recognized and trusted as a reliable currency, further enhancing its potential to serve as a reserve currency in the global financial system.

While XRP has some strengths that make it a potential candidate for a reserve currency, it also faces several challenges and hurdles to overcome:

Competition: XRP is not the only cryptocurrency aiming to become a reserve currency. Other major cryptocurrencies, such as Bitcoin and Ethereum, are also competing for this status. Each of these cryptocurrencies has its strengths and weaknesses, making it difficult to predict which, if any, will eventually become a widely accepted reserve currency.

Regulatory Uncertainty: The regulatory environment around cryptocurrencies is still evolving. Governments and financial institutions around the world are in the process of developing rules and regulations to govern the use of cryptocurrencies like XRP. Regulatory uncertainty could hinder XRP's progress toward becoming a reserve currency, as businesses and individuals may be hesitant to adopt it if the regulatory landscape remains unclear.

Volatility: Cryptocurrencies, including XRP, are known for their price volatility. This can be a significant drawback for a reserve currency, as it should ideally have a stable value to serve as a reliable store of wealth. XRP's volatility may deter central banks and other institutions from holding it as a reserve currency.

Adoption and Acceptance: Although XRP has seen significant growth in its network and acceptance worldwide, it still lags behind traditional reserve currencies like the US dollar and the euro. For XRP to become a viable reserve currency, it must achieve a level of adoption and acceptance that rivals these established currencies.

Trust and Perception: Trust is an essential component of any reserve currency. People and institutions must believe that the currency is reliable and secure. Cryptocurrencies, including XRP, are still relatively new and can be perceived as risky or unstable by some. Overcoming this perception and building trust in XRP will be crucial for it to become a widely accepted reserve currency.

While XRP has some qualities that make it a potential candidate for a reserve currency, it faces several challenges and hurdles it must overcome. These include competition from other cryptocurrencies, regulatory uncertainty, price volatility, adoption and acceptance, and building trust and perception.

15.5 Comparing XRP to Other Reserve Currency Contenders

When comparing XRP to other reserve currency contenders, it's important to consider various factors, such as speed, scalability, cost efficiency, decentralization, and security. Let's take a look at how XRP compares to some of the other major cryptocurrencies:

XRP vs. Bitcoin (BTC):

Speed and Scalability: XRP is significantly faster and more scalable than Bitcoin. While XRP can process up to 1,500 transactions per second with a settlement time of around 3-5 seconds, Bitcoin can handle only about 7 transactions per second with an average settlement time of 10 minutes or more.

Cost Efficiency: XRP's transaction fees are much lower than those of Bitcoin. XRP fees typically range from a fraction of a penny to a few cents, while Bitcoin fees can be several dollars or even higher during periods of high network congestion.

Decentralization and Security: While both XRP and Bitcoin are decentralized, Bitcoin is often seen as more decentralized due to its proof-of-work consensus mechanism. However, XRP's consensus mechanism allows for better energy efficiency and lower environmental impact compared to Bitcoin's energy-intensive mining process.

XRP vs. Ethereum (ETH):

Speed and Scalability: XRP is faster and more scalable than Ethereum. Ethereum can handle about 30 transactions per second with varying settlement times, while XRP can process up to 1,500 transactions per second with near-instant settlement.

Cost Efficiency: XRP's transaction fees are generally lower than Ethereum's, which can become quite high during periods of network congestion due to its gas fee system.

Decentralization and Security: Both XRP and Ethereum are decentralized, but Ethereum is currently transitioning from a proof-of-work to a proof-of-stake consensus mechanism, which will make it more energy-efficient and environmentally friendly. XRP's consensus mechanism is already energy-efficient.

XRP vs. Stablecoins (USDT, USDC, etc.):

Speed and Scalability: XRP is generally faster and more scalable than most stablecoins, which often rely on the Ethereum network or other slower blockchains.

Cost Efficiency: XRP's transaction fees are typically lower than those associated with stablecoin transactions, especially those that rely on the Ethereum network.

Stability: One key advantage that stablecoins have over XRP is their price stability. Stablecoins are pegged to a reserve of assets, such as the US dollar or other fiat currencies, which helps maintain a stable value. XRP, like most cryptocurrencies, can be volatile.

XRP has some advantages over other reserve currency contenders, such as speed, scalability, and cost efficiency. However, it also faces challenges, like competition from other cryptocurrencies, price volatility, and perceptions of decentralization and security.

16.1 Understanding the Differences: Securities, Currencies, and Commodities

To understand the debate around XRP's classification, it's important to know the differences between securities, currencies, and commodities. Let's break down each of these terms:

Securities: Securities are financial instruments that represent ownership in a company or an obligation to repay debt. Common types of securities include stocks, bonds, and mutual funds. Securities are regulated by government agencies, such as the U.S. Securities and Exchange Commission (SEC), to protect investors and ensure fair market practices.

Currencies: Currencies are mediums of exchange used to facilitate transactions between parties. They are typically issued by governments and central banks and are accepted as legal tender within a specific geographic region. Examples of currencies include the U.S. dollar, the Euro, and the Japanese yen. Currencies are regulated by central banks and other government agencies responsible for managing monetary policy.

Commodities: Commodities are raw materials or primary products that can be bought, sold, or traded in various markets. They are typically used as inputs in the production of goods or services. Examples of commodities include crude oil, gold, and agricultural products like wheat and corn. Commodities are traded in specialized markets, and their prices are generally determined by supply and demand factors.

XRP's classification has been a subject of debate, as it exhibits characteristics of all three categories. As a digital asset, it can be used as a medium of exchange (like a currency) and has features that make it useful for cross-border transactions and remittances. At the same time, it is also used to facilitate transactions on the Ripple network, which could be seen as a utility or commodity. Finally, some argue that XRP could be considered a security because it was initially distributed by Ripple Labs and may be perceived as an investment in the company's success.

The classification of XRP has significant implications for its regulation, taxation, and overall treatment within the financial system. Different jurisdictions may classify XRP differently, leading to varying levels of regulatory scrutiny and compliance requirements for users and businesses dealing with XRP.

To better understand XRP's classification, let's examine its unique characteristics and how they relate to securities, currencies, and commodities.

Medium of Exchange: XRP can be used as a medium of exchange, facilitating transactions between parties. Its fast transaction times and low fees make it an attractive option for cross-border payments and remittances. This characteristic aligns with the typical functions of a currency.

Decentralization: Although Ripple Labs created XRP, the XRP Ledger operates on a decentralized network, meaning no single entity has complete control over it. This decentralization aspect differs from traditional securities, which typically represent ownership or control over a centralized company or organization.

Utility and Use Cases: XRP has several use cases, such as facilitating transactions on the Ripple network, providing liquidity to financial institutions, and supporting micropayments. These utilities make XRP more akin to a commodity, as its value is derived from its functionality and use in various applications.

Initial Distribution: XRP was initially distributed by Ripple Labs, with a portion of the total supply retained by the company. This distribution method has led some to argue that XRP could be considered a security because investors may have purchased it with the expectation of profiting from the success of Ripple Labs.

Market Behavior: XRP's price tends to fluctuate based on market demand, similar to commodities and currencies. This price behavior differs from securities, which are often more directly influenced by the financial performance and prospects of the issuing company.

Regulatory Approvals: In some jurisdictions, XRP has been recognized as a currency or commodity, while in others, it has been subject to regulatory scrutiny as a potential security. This inconsistency highlights the ongoing debate surrounding XRP's classification and the need for clearer regulatory guidance.

Given these characteristics, XRP does not fit neatly into any one category. It shares traits with currencies, commodities, and securities, making its classification a complex and evolving issue. As the digital asset landscape continues to develop, regulators and market participants will need to consider these unique features when determining the appropriate treatment of XRP and other similar digital assets.

16.2.1 Security: Does XRP Meet the Criteria?

To determine if XRP meets the criteria to be classified as a security, we can refer to the Howey Test, a commonly used method for evaluating whether an asset is a security. The Howey Test has four key components:

Investment of Money: An investment of money is required for something to be considered a security. In the case of XRP, people can buy and sell it using fiat or other cryptocurrencies, fulfilling this criterion.

Common Enterprise: A common enterprise refers to a venture in which investors pool their resources to achieve a shared goal. While XRP was initially distributed by Ripple Labs, it operates on a decentralized network, and the value of XRP is not directly tied to the success or failure of the company. This aspect makes it challenging to determine if XRP meets the common enterprise criterion.

Expectation of Profits: For an asset to be considered a security, there must be an expectation of profits primarily from the efforts of others. Although some XRP holders may anticipate profits from the asset's appreciation, the value of XRP is driven by market demand, its utility, and overall adoption, rather than the actions of Ripple Labs alone. This characteristic makes the expectation of profits criterion debatable in the case of XRP.

Efforts of a Promoter or Third Party: Lastly, the profits generated must come from the efforts of a promoter or a third party. While Ripple Labs has played a significant role in developing and promoting XRP, the decentralized nature of the XRP Ledger means that the network is not under the control of Ripple Labs. This decentralization aspect complicates whether XRP meets this criterion.

XRP's classification as a security remains uncertain, as it does not clearly satisfy all the criteria outlined in the Howey Test. While XRP meets some of the requirements, its decentralized nature and the fact that its value is not directly tied to the success of Ripple Labs make it challenging to definitively categorize it as a security. This ambiguity highlights the need for clearer regulatory guidance and understanding of digital assets like XRP.

16.2.2 Currency: XRP's Functionality as a Medium of Exchange

A currency is a widely accepted form of money that serves as a medium of exchange, a unit of account, and a store of value. Let's explore how XRP performs in these roles:

Medium of Exchange: As a digital asset, XRP can be used to transfer value across borders quickly and at a low cost. Its fast transaction processing times (3-5 seconds) and low transaction fees make it well-suited for cross-border payments, remittances, and other financial applications. XRP's use in Ripple's On-Demand Liquidity (ODL) service exemplifies its effectiveness as a medium of exchange.

Unit of Account: A unit of account is a standard measure used to express the value of goods and services. XRP, like other cryptocurrencies, can be used as a unit of account, with its value expressed in terms of other currencies, such as US dollars or euros. However, it is essential to note that XRP's value can be volatile, which may affect its practicality as a stable unit of account.

Store of Value: A store of value is an asset that can maintain its worth over time. While XRP has shown potential as a store of value, its price volatility, similar to other cryptocurrencies, may pose challenges in maintaining a consistent value over extended periods. Despite this, many investors and users hold XRP with the expectation that its value will appreciate over time.

XRP exhibits several characteristics of a currency, primarily in its functionality as a medium of exchange. However, its price volatility can impact its effectiveness as a stable unit of account and store of value. As the digital asset ecosystem matures and XRP continues to be adopted for various use cases, it may further solidify its position as a form of digital currency.

16.2.3 Commodity: Assessing XRP's Commodity-like Features

A commodity is a basic good or raw material that is interchangeable with other goods of the same type. It typically has value and can be traded in the marketplace. Let's examine XRP's features that resemble a commodity:

Fungibility: Fungibility is the property of an asset where individual units are interchangeable and indistinguishable from one another. XRP, like other cryptocurrencies, is fungible, as one XRP token has the same value and utility as any other XRP token. This characteristic is similar to commodities like gold, where one ounce of gold can be exchanged for another ounce of gold.

Tradable: XRP is a tradable asset, with its value determined by market forces. It can be bought, sold, or exchanged for other cryptocurrencies and fiat currencies on various trading platforms. This ability to be traded is a feature common to commodities.

Utility: Commodities often have a specific utility or use case. In the case of XRP, its primary utility lies in facilitating cross-border transactions and acting as a bridge currency in Ripple's payment solutions. This practical application of XRP resembles the utility aspect of commodities.

Store of Value: While XRP's price can be volatile, many investors and users hold it as a store of value, anticipating its price to appreciate over time. This aspect is similar to commodities like gold or silver, which are often held as stores of value.

XRP exhibits several commodity-like features, such as fungibility, tradability, utility, and the potential to act as a store of value. Although XRP's classification as a security, currency, or commodity may still be debated, understanding its various characteristics can help users and investors make informed decisions about its potential use cases and value.

16.3 Regulatory Perspectives on XRP Classification

Regulatory perspectives on XRP classification vary across different jurisdictions and regulatory bodies. This can have implications for how XRP is treated for taxation, legal, and compliance purposes. Let's look at some regulatory viewpoints:

United States: In the U.S., the Securities and Exchange Commission (SEC) has an ongoing lawsuit against Ripple Labs, claiming that XRP is an unregistered security. However, the Financial Crimes Enforcement Network (FinCEN) has previously classified XRP as a virtual currency. The Commodity Futures Trading Commission (CFTC) has not explicitly classified XRP, but it generally views cryptocurrencies as commodities. This ongoing debate highlights the lack of a unified regulatory stance on XRP in the U.S.

United Kingdom: The UK's Financial Conduct Authority (FCA) classifies XRP as a utility/exchange token rather than a security. This classification groups XRP with other cryptocurrencies like Bitcoin and Ethereum, which the FCA also considers utility/exchange tokens.

Japan: Japan's Financial Services Agency (FSA) views XRP as a cryptocurrency, and not a security. This position is significant because Ripple Labs has strong ties with Japanese financial institutions and has expressed interest in potentially relocating its headquarters to Japan.

Other Countries: Regulatory perspectives on XRP vary globally, with some countries viewing it as a digital asset, others as a virtual currency, and some not providing any explicit classification.

There is no unified global regulatory stance on XRP classification, with different countries and regulatory bodies having their own perspectives. This lack of consensus can create challenges for XRP users and investors when it comes to legal compliance and taxation. It is essential for individuals and businesses dealing with XRP to stay informed about the regulatory environment in their respective jurisdictions and to consult with professionals when necessary.

16.3.1 United States: The SEC's Stance and Ongoing Litigation

In the United States, the Securities and Exchange Commission (SEC) is responsible for regulating securities markets and protecting investors. The SEC has been involved in an ongoing lawsuit with Ripple Labs, the company behind XRP, since December 2020.

The crux of the SEC's argument is that XRP should be classified as a security, specifically an unregistered security. According to the SEC, Ripple Labs and its executives have raised over $1.3 billion through an unregistered, ongoing digital asset securities offering. The SEC claims that XRP was sold to investors with the expectation of profit, largely based on the efforts of Ripple Labs to develop the XRP ecosystem and drive up the value of the token. In the SEC's view, this makes XRP a security and subject to securities laws.

Ripple Labs, on the other hand, argues that XRP is not a security but a digital asset or cryptocurrency. They contend that XRP functions as a medium of exchange and does not represent an ownership stake in the company. Ripple Labs also points out that the SEC's stance on XRP is inconsistent with its views on Bitcoin and Ethereum, which the SEC has deemed not to be securities.

The outcome of this legal battle between the SEC and Ripple Labs is still uncertain, with both parties presenting their cases in court. The final decision could have significant implications for the XRP ecosystem, as well as for the broader cryptocurrency industry in the United States.

For now, it is crucial for individuals and businesses dealing with XRP to be aware of this ongoing legal situation and to consult with legal or financial professionals to ensure compliance with applicable regulations.

16.3.2 International Perspectives: Diverging Regulatory Approaches

While the United States is grappling with the classification of XRP, other countries around the world have taken various approaches to regulating cryptocurrencies, including XRP. Some nations have classified XRP as a currency or digital asset, while others have opted for a more cautious approach by classifying it as a security or implementing strict regulations.

Japan: The Japanese Financial Services Agency (FSA) has been progressive in its approach to cryptocurrencies, recognizing them as legal property since 2017. XRP, in particular, has been classified as a cryptocurrency and not a security in Japan. This favorable regulatory environment has allowed XRP and other cryptocurrencies to thrive in the country.

United Kingdom: The UK's Financial Conduct Authority (FCA) has not classified XRP as a security. Instead, it considers XRP to be a digital asset or "exchange token." This classification means that XRP is not subject to the same regulations as securities, making it easier for businesses and investors to work with XRP in the UK.

European Union: The European Union has not adopted a uniform approach to the classification of cryptocurrencies. However, individual member states have their interpretations and approaches to regulating digital assets. For instance, in countries like Germany and France, XRP is considered a digital asset and not a security.

Switzerland: The Swiss Financial Market Supervisory Authority (FINMA) has been proactive in developing a regulatory framework for cryptocurrencies. While it does not explicitly classify XRP, it has created a category called "payment tokens," which XRP may fall under, treating it as a digital asset rather than a security.

India: The regulatory landscape in India is uncertain, with the government considering various approaches to cryptocurrency regulation. While there is no explicit classification of XRP, the Reserve Bank of India (RBI) has expressed concerns about cryptocurrencies and has attempted to implement restrictions on their use in the past.

The classification of XRP varies from country to country, with some nations embracing it as a digital asset or currency, while others remain cautious or undecided. The regulatory landscape for XRP and cryptocurrencies, in general, is constantly evolving. It is essential for individuals and businesses dealing with XRP to be aware of the regulations in their specific jurisdictions and stay updated on any changes to ensure compliance.

16.4 Implications of XRP's Classification for Investors and Users

The classification of XRP as a security, currency, or commodity can have significant implications for both investors and users. Here's an overview of the potential consequences for each classification:

Security:

If XRP were classified as a security, it would be subject to strict regulations and reporting requirements. This could impact businesses working with XRP and potentially limit the token's usage.

Investors would need to comply with securities laws, which could involve additional paperwork and restrictions on trading and holding XRP.

Exchanges listing XRP might need to register as securities exchanges or remove XRP from their platform to avoid regulatory penalties, potentially reducing liquidity and access to the token.

Currency:

If XRP were recognized as a currency, it would likely be subject to fewer regulations and reporting requirements than securities.

Users could potentially benefit from lower transaction costs and more accessible financial services, as XRP would be recognized as a legitimate means of payment and value transfer.

Exchanges and businesses working with XRP would have an easier time complying with regulations, making it simpler for them to incorporate XRP into their operations.

Commodity:

If XRP were classified as a commodity, it would fall under the jurisdiction of a different set of regulations, which might be less stringent than those for securities.

Exchanges and businesses could face fewer regulatory hurdles, making it easier for them to work with XRP.

Users and investors might have a wider range of options for trading and investing in XRP, as commodities can be traded on various platforms and are subject to different rules than securities.

The classification of XRP can significantly impact how it is regulated, traded, and used. Each classification comes with its unique set of advantages and challenges, so it is essential for investors and users to keep track of the ongoing developments and adjust their strategies accordingly.

16.5 The Future of XRP Classification and Its Impact on the Ecosystem

The future of XRP's classification remains uncertain, but its eventual determination will have significant implications for the entire XRP ecosystem. Here's an overview of the potential impacts:

Legal clarity and regulatory certainty:

An official classification of XRP would provide much-needed clarity for businesses, investors, and users. This clarity would help reduce the risks associated with regulatory uncertainty and facilitate more informed decision-making.

A clear classification could also lead to better-defined regulations, enabling companies working with XRP to comply more easily and ensure they operate within legal bounds.

Innovation and growth:
A favorable classification, such as currency or commodity, could stimulate innovation and growth within the XRP ecosystem. This would encourage more businesses to adopt and build on XRP, leading to the development of new products, services, and use cases.

However, a more restrictive classification, like security, might hinder innovation by imposing strict regulations and reporting requirements, which could discourage companies from working with XRP.

Adoption and market penetration:

A clear and favorable classification would likely boost XRP's adoption, as it would be recognized as a legitimate financial instrument. This could lead to increased market penetration, with more businesses and individuals using XRP for various purposes, such as remittances, payments, and investment.

On the other hand, a restrictive classification could limit XRP's adoption and market penetration, as businesses and individuals might be more hesitant to engage with a heavily regulated asset.

Market stability and investor confidence:

The resolution of XRP's classification debate could bring stability to the market and restore investor confidence. A clear regulatory framework would provide assurance to investors and users, making them more comfortable participating in the XRP ecosystem.

However, an unfavorable classification might have the opposite effect, causing market volatility and potentially diminishing investor confidence in XRP.

The future of XRP's classification will significantly impact the ecosystem's growth, adoption, and stability. It is crucial for stakeholders, including businesses, investors, and users, to monitor the ongoing legal and regulatory developments to navigate the evolving landscape and make informed decisions.

Chapter 17: Advanced XRP Trading Strategies
17.1 Understanding Cryptocurrency Trading Basics

Cryptocurrency trading involves the buying, selling, and exchange of digital assets like XRP. It's an activity that can be quite profitable, but also risky, given the volatile nature of cryptocurrency markets. Therefore, understanding the basic principles of cryptocurrency trading is essential before diving into advanced trading strategies.

Trading cryptocurrencies, including XRP, involves several fundamental concepts that you need to comprehend to successfully navigate the digital asset market.

Cryptocurrency Exchanges

Cryptocurrency exchanges are platforms where you can buy, sell, and trade cryptocurrencies. These platforms are vital in the trading process. They provide the necessary infrastructure for traders to interact with the cryptocurrency market. Examples include Binance, Kraken, Coinbase, and Bitstamp. Each exchange has different features, fees, security measures, and supported cryptocurrencies. It's crucial to choose an exchange that best fits your trading needs and objectives.

Trading Pairs

Trading pairs are a fundamental concept in cryptocurrency trading. They represent two different types of cryptocurrencies that can be exchanged for one another on a trading platform. For example, a trading pair could be XRP/USD, where XRP is the base currency, and USD is the quote currency. This pair indicates that you can buy or sell XRP for USD.

Order Types

Understanding different order types is crucial for effective trading. The most basic types are 'market' and 'limit' orders. A market order is a request to buy or sell a cryptocurrency immediately at the best available price. A limit order, on the other hand, is a request to buy or sell a cryptocurrency at a specific price or better. Other advanced order types include 'stop loss' and 'take profit' orders, which are designed to limit losses and secure profits respectively.

Trading Volume and Liquidity

Trading volume is the total amount of a specific cryptocurrency that has been traded in a given period. High trading volumes often indicate a high interest in the asset and can lead to price volatility. Liquidity, on the other hand, refers to the ease with which a cryptocurrency can be bought or sold without causing significant price changes. High liquidity is generally desirable in trading as it allows for easier entry and exit from positions.

Price Volatility

Cryptocurrencies, including XRP, are known for their price volatility. This is the rate at which the price of a crypto asset increases or decreases for a set of returns. Volatility is measured by calculating the standard deviation of the annualized returns over a given period of time. High volatility means that a crypto asset can potentially be spread over a large range of values. This can be both an opportunity for traders for potential trading profits and a risk.

Slippage

Slippage is another important concept in cryptocurrency trading. It refers to the difference between the expected price of a trade and the price at which the trade is executed. Slippage can occur during periods of high volatility when market orders are used, and also when large orders are executed when there isn't enough volume at the chosen price.

Cryptocurrency Wallets

Cryptocurrency wallets are tools that allow you to store and manage your digital assets. They come in various forms, including software, hardware, and paper wallets. It's crucial to understand how to use and secure your cryptocurrency wallets, as they are responsible for storing your traded assets.

Blockchain and Transaction Verification

Cryptocurrencies operate on blockchain technology. A blockchain is a decentralized and distributed digital ledger that records transactions across multiple computers. Understanding how blockchain works is fundamental to understanding how transactions are verified and recorded in the cryptocurrency world.

All these elements form the basis of cryptocurrency trading. Understanding them is crucial for any trader who wishes to engage in advanced XRP trading strategies. It's important to remember that cryptocurrency trading involves significant risks and isn't suitable for everyone. Therefore, it's recommended to thoroughly research and consider your financial situation before venturing into cryptocurrency trading.

Technical analysis is a popular approach used by traders to analyze and predict the future price movements of financial assets, including cryptocurrencies like XRP. It involves studying historical price patterns and trading volumes to identify potential trends, support and resistance levels, and other market indicators. The goal is to make informed decisions on when to enter or exit a trade based on these insights.

Here are some essential components of technical analysis for XRP trading:

Chart Types

There are various chart types used in technical analysis, with the most common being line, bar, and candlestick charts. Each chart type represents price data differently and serves a unique purpose in analyzing market trends. For example, candlestick charts provide more information about price movements within a specific time frame, making them particularly useful for short-term trading.

Trend Analysis

Trend analysis is the process of identifying the general direction of the market (upward, downward, or sideways) based on historical price data. In technical analysis, trends are considered the foundation for making trading decisions. Traders use various tools, such as trendlines and moving averages, to identify and analyze trends. Recognizing and following trends can help traders make more informed decisions about when to enter or exit positions.

Support and Resistance Levels

Support and resistance levels are crucial concepts in technical analysis. Support levels represent a price point where buying pressure is expected to be strong enough to prevent further price decline. Resistance levels, on the other hand, represent a price point where selling pressure is expected to be strong enough to prevent further price increase. Identifying these levels can help traders determine entry and exit points for their trades.

Technical Indicators

Technical indicators are mathematical calculations based on price, volume, or open interest data, which aim to provide a visual representation of market trends and conditions. There are various types of technical indicators, including trend indicators, momentum indicators, volatility indicators, and volume indicators. Some commonly used indicators in XRP trading include the Moving Average Convergence Divergence (MACD), Relative Strength Index (RSI), Bollinger Bands, and Fibonacci Retracement levels.

Pattern Recognition

Pattern recognition involves identifying specific price patterns that tend to repeat themselves in the market. These patterns, such as head and shoulders, double tops/bottoms, and flags, can provide valuable insights into potential price movements. Learning to recognize and interpret these patterns can help traders make better-informed trading decisions.

Timeframes

Technical analysis can be applied to different timeframes, depending on the trader's goals and strategies. Short-term traders, such as day traders and scalpers, may focus on shorter timeframes (e.g., 1-minute or 5-minute charts) to identify and exploit short-term price movements. Long-term traders, such as swing traders and position traders, may use longer timeframes (e.g., daily or weekly charts) to analyze and trade on broader market trends.

Backtesting

Backtesting is an essential process in technical analysis that involves testing a trading strategy on historical data to evaluate its performance. This can help traders refine their strategies, identify potential weaknesses, and gain more confidence in their trading decisions. Many trading platforms offer backtesting tools to help traders analyze their strategies before implementing them in live trading.

Technical analysis is an invaluable tool for XRP traders looking to capitalize on market trends and price movements. By understanding and applying various technical analysis concepts and tools, traders can make more informed decisions about when to enter or exit trades, potentially increasing their chances of success in the volatile world of cryptocurrency trading.

17.3 Fundamental Analysis in the Context of XRP

Fundamental analysis is a method used by traders to evaluate the intrinsic value of an asset by examining its underlying factors and drivers. In the context of XRP, fundamental analysis involves assessing various aspects of the Ripple ecosystem, such as its technology, partnerships, regulatory environment, and market competition. The goal is to determine whether XRP is undervalued or overvalued based on these factors, providing a basis for informed trading decisions.

Here are some essential components of fundamental analysis for XRP trading:

Ripple's Technology and Use Cases

The first step in conducting fundamental analysis on XRP is to understand Ripple's technology and its use cases. Ripple's primary product, RippleNet, is a decentralized global payments network that aims to enable instant, secure, and low-cost cross-border transactions. The native cryptocurrency, XRP, is used as a bridge currency within

RippleNet, facilitating the exchange of different currencies and improving liquidity.

Understanding the benefits of Ripple's technology, such as faster transaction times, lower fees, and scalability, can help traders assess the potential value of XRP in the context of the global financial system.

Partnerships and Adoption

A crucial aspect of fundamental analysis for XRP is examining the partnerships Ripple has established with various financial institutions, payment providers, and businesses. These partnerships can indicate the level of adoption and acceptance of Ripple's technology in the market. Additionally, it's essential to monitor new partnerships, as they may have a significant impact on the demand and value of XRP.

Regulatory Environment

The regulatory environment plays a critical role in the adoption and success of cryptocurrencies, including XRP. Understanding the regulatory stance of different countries and how it might affect Ripple's operations and adoption is essential for fundamental analysis. This includes monitoring any legal developments, such as lawsuits or regulatory changes, which might impact Ripple and XRP's value.

Market Competition

Analyzing the competitive landscape of the cryptocurrency market is another vital component of fundamental analysis. Assessing XRP's competitors, such as other cryptocurrencies or traditional financial systems, can help traders understand its potential market share and growth prospects. Keeping an eye on developments and innovations in the market can provide insights into XRP's competitive advantages or disadvantages.

Market Sentiment and News

Market sentiment and news play a significant role in influencing the value of cryptocurrencies. Monitoring news related to Ripple, XRP, and the broader cryptocurrency industry can help traders stay informed about developments that may impact XRP's price. This includes announcements, partnerships, regulatory updates, and technology advancements.

XRP Supply and Distribution

Examining XRP's supply and distribution is an essential aspect of fundamental analysis. XRP has a total supply of 100 billion tokens, with a significant portion held by Ripple Labs and its founders. Understanding the distribution and release schedule of XRP tokens can help traders anticipate potential changes in supply that may affect the asset's price.

Fundamental analysis in the context of XRP involves examining various aspects of the Ripple ecosystem to determine the cryptocurrency's intrinsic value. By considering factors such as technology, partnerships, regulatory environment, and market competition, traders can make more informed decisions about whether to invest in XRP or not. Combining fundamental analysis with technical analysis can provide a comprehensive approach to XRP trading, potentially increasing the chances of success in the volatile world of cryptocurrency trading.

17.4 Trading XRP Futures and Derivatives

Trading XRP futures and derivatives is a more advanced aspect of cryptocurrency trading that allows traders to capitalize on market movements without actually owning the underlying asset. It provides opportunities for hedging, leverage, and speculation that are not available in traditional spot trading.

Futures

A futures contract is an agreement to buy or sell an asset at a predetermined price at a specified future date. In the context of XRP, futures trading allows traders to speculate on the future price of XRP without owning the actual cryptocurrency. Traders can make profits by correctly predicting whether the price of XRP will rise or fall by the contract's expiration date.

One of the main benefits of futures trading is the ability to use leverage. Leverage allows traders to open positions larger than their initial capital. While this can amplify profits, it can also amplify losses if the market moves against the trader's position, making it a risky strategy that requires careful risk management.

Futures contracts for XRP are available on several cryptocurrency exchanges, including Binance, BitMEX, and Kraken. Each exchange has different contract specifications, such as contract size, expiration dates, and leverage options, so it's important for traders to familiarize themselves with these details before trading.

Options

Options are another type of derivative that gives the buyer the right, but not the obligation, to buy or sell an asset at a predetermined price within a specific time frame. There are two types of options: call options (which give the right to buy) and put options (which give the right to sell).

Options trading can be used for various strategies, including hedging, speculation, and generating income. However, options trading is complex and involves high risk, making it suitable for more experienced traders.

Swaps

Cryptocurrency swaps are another type of derivative in which two parties agree to exchange sequences of cash flows for a set period. The most common type of swap in cryptocurrency trading is a perpetual swap, which is similar to a futures contract but has no expiration date.

Perpetual swaps can be used to speculate on long-term price movements of XRP, and they often come with a funding rate that traders pay or receive, depending on the position they hold.

Contracts for Difference (CFDs)

CFDs are derivatives that allow traders to speculate on the price movements of XRP without owning the actual cryptocurrency. When trading a CFD, a trader merely speculates on the rise or fall of the XRP price within the contract duration.

However, it's important to note that CFDs are complex instruments and come with a high risk of losing money rapidly due to leverage. Also, in some jurisdictions, trading CFDs on cryptocurrencies is restricted or prohibited due to regulatory reasons.

In conclusion, trading XRP futures and other derivatives can offer advanced trading strategies and greater financial flexibility compared to traditional spot trading. However, these instruments are complex and involve significant risks, including the risk of losing the entire investment. Therefore, they should be used with caution and appropriate risk management strategies. It's recommended for traders to thoroughly understand these instruments and consider their risk tolerance before venturing into XRP futures and derivatives trading.

Risk management is a critical aspect of any trading strategy, particularly in the volatile world of cryptocurrencies like XRP. Without proper risk management, traders may expose themselves to unnecessary risks, potentially leading to substantial losses. Here are some key risk management strategies that traders should consider when trading XRP:

Setting Stop-Loss and Take-Profit Orders

Stop-loss and take-profit orders are essential tools for managing risk. A stop-loss order automatically closes a position when the price reaches a predetermined level to prevent further losses. Conversely, a take-profit order closes a position once the price reaches a predetermined level to lock in profits. These orders can help traders manage their risk by ensuring that they don't lose more than they're willing to or miss out on taking profits when they're available.

Position Sizing

Position sizing refers to the size of a trade relative to the trader's total portfolio. It's a crucial part of risk management because it determines the amount of risk a trader is taking on with each trade. A common rule of thumb is to risk no more than 1-2% of the total portfolio on a single trade, although this can vary depending on the trader's risk tolerance and trading strategy.

Diversification

Diversification involves spreading investments across various assets to reduce the impact of a single asset's performance on the overall portfolio. In the context of XRP trading, this could mean diversifying into other cryptocurrencies or even other asset classes like stocks, bonds, or commodities.

Leverage Management

Leverage allows traders to open positions larger than their initial capital, potentially amplifying profits. However, it also amplifies losses, making it a double-edged sword. Traders must be careful when using leverage, as it can lead to substantial losses if the market moves against their position. It's essential to understand the risks involved and to use leverage judiciously.

Regularly Reviewing and Adjusting the Trading Strategy

Market conditions can change rapidly, and a trading strategy that worked well in the past may not work as well in the future. Regularly reviewing and adjusting the trading strategy based on current market conditions and performance can help manage risk over time.

Emotional Control

Trading can be an emotional endeavor, and emotions like fear and greed can lead to poor decision-making. Developing emotional control and sticking to the trading plan, even when emotions are running high, is a critical part of risk management.

Continued Learning and Education

The cryptocurrency market is continuously evolving, and staying up-to-date with the latest developments, technologies, and regulations can help manage risk. This includes not only learning about XRP and its ecosystem but also about broader market trends and other cryptocurrencies.

Risk management is an essential part of XRP trading. By implementing effective risk management strategies, traders can better manage their exposure and potentially improve their trading outcomes. It's important to remember that while these strategies can help manage risk, they can't eliminate it entirely. Therefore, only risk capital that you can afford to lose should be used for trading.

Chapter 18: XRP's role in the evolving cryptocurrency regulatory landscape

As of mid-2023, cryptocurrency regulation is a rapidly evolving and complex area. Different countries have various approaches, ranging from embracing digital assets and blockchain technology to outright bans. This regulatory landscape significantly impacts the adoption, price, and development of cryptocurrencies like XRP.

United States

In the United States, cryptocurrencies are primarily regulated as securities, commodities, or property, depending on their characteristics. The Securities and Exchange Commission (SEC) oversees those classified as securities, while the Commodity Futures Trading Commission (CFTC) regulates those deemed commodities. If treated as property, cryptocurrencies are subject to capital gains tax.

However, the regulatory environment is complex and somewhat fragmented due to various federal and state-level regulations. Regulatory clarity on cryptocurrencies, including XRP, is still sought after by many in the industry, leading to ongoing discussions and legal disputes.

European Union

In the European Union, the regulatory approach towards cryptocurrencies has been generally positive, with efforts made to foster innovation while mitigating risks. The proposed Markets in Crypto-Assets (MiCA) regulation, which aims to provide a comprehensive framework for crypto-assets across the EU, is a significant development. However, the regulation does not classify cryptocurrencies, leaving it to individual member states, which leads to a diverse range of approaches.

Asia

In Asia, the regulatory landscape is varied. Some countries, like Singapore and South Korea, have implemented comprehensive regulatory frameworks that encourage crypto innovation while managing risks. China, on the other hand, has taken a stricter stance, cracking down on cryptocurrency trading and mining activities.

In Japan, cryptocurrencies are recognized as legal property, and exchanges are required to register with the Financial Services Agency. India, however, has been in regulatory flux with shifting stances on the legality and regulation of cryptocurrencies.

Emerging Economies

In many emerging economies, cryptocurrencies are seen as a means of financial inclusion and a way to bypass inefficient or unstable local financial systems. Countries like Nigeria, Kenya, and Venezuela have high cryptocurrency adoption rates. However, regulatory approaches in these countries vary widely, with some governments imposing restrictions due to concerns over financial stability and illicit activities.

In conclusion, the current state of cryptocurrency regulation worldwide is highly varied and rapidly evolving. The lack of a consistent global regulatory framework leads to significant uncertainty and poses challenges for cryptocurrencies, including XRP. How individual countries choose to regulate cryptocurrencies can significantly impact their adoption, use cases, and value. Therefore, keeping abreast of regulatory developments is crucial for anyone involved in the cryptocurrency space.

18.2 How Regulations Have Shaped XRP and Ripple's Strategies

Regulatory considerations have significantly influenced the development of XRP and Ripple's strategies, causing Ripple to adjust its operations and goals to meet the evolving regulatory landscape. This section will explore some of the ways that regulatory influences have impacted XRP and Ripple.

Legal Classification of XRP

One of the most significant regulatory challenges for XRP has been the question of its legal classification. Depending on jurisdiction, cryptocurrencies can be classified as commodities, securities, or property, which significantly impacts how they can be used and traded.

In the United States, the SEC's decision to sue Ripple Labs in December 2020, alleging that XRP was a security and that Ripple had conducted an unregistered securities offering, was a significant development. This lawsuit has had considerable effects on XRP's price and Ripple's business operations, leading to a temporary suspension of XRP trading on many U.S. exchanges and causing Ripple to consider moving its headquarters out of the U.S.

Global Expansion and Partnerships

Regulatory considerations have also guided Ripple's global expansion and partnership strategies. Ripple has actively sought partnerships in countries with more favourable or clear regulatory environments for cryptocurrencies, such as Japan and the United Arab Emirates.

For instance, Ripple has established significant relationships with financial institutions in Japan, a country known for its progressive stance towards cryptocurrencies. Additionally, Ripple's acquisition of a 40% stake in Asia's leading cross-border payment specialist, Tranglo, is an example of strategic expansion to regions with a supportive regulatory environment.

Development of RippleNet and On-Demand Liquidity

Ripple's development of RippleNet and the On-Demand Liquidity (ODL) service has also been influenced by regulatory considerations. RippleNet, a global payments network that allows financial institutions to connect and transfer money globally, was designed to be compliant with existing financial regulations, making it more appealing to regulated financial institutions.

ODL, which uses XRP as a bridge currency for cross-border transactions, was developed in part to circumvent traditional banking systems' inefficiencies, some of which are due to regulatory constraints. However, the adoption of ODL by financial institutions can also be impacted by the regulatory environment surrounding XRP.

Engagement with Regulators and Policy Makers

Recognizing the importance of regulatory clarity for the success of its business model, Ripple has been proactive in engaging with regulators and policymakers around the world. Ripple has consistently advocated for a clear, fair, and comprehensive regulatory framework for cryptocurrencies in the U.S. and globally.

The evolving regulatory landscape has significantly shaped XRP and Ripple's strategies. Navigating these regulations has proven to be a considerable challenge, but it has also led to innovation and strategic decisions that could position Ripple and XRP for success in the increasingly regulated world of cryptocurrencies.

Global regulatory trends significantly influence the status, adoption, and utility of cryptocurrencies like XRP. Understanding these trends and their potential impacts on XRP is crucial for anyone involved in XRP trading or usage.

Increased Regulatory Clarity

The global trend toward increased regulatory clarity is positive for XRP. As more countries provide clear rules and guidelines for cryptocurrency trading and usage, it creates a more stable environment for cryptocurrencies. Clarity can also open up more use cases, as businesses and financial institutions are more likely to adopt cryptocurrencies when they understand the legal and regulatory implications.

For example, in Japan, where the regulatory environment is relatively clear, XRP has seen significant adoption. Financial institutions have partnered with Ripple for cross-border payments, and XRP is listed on several Japanese cryptocurrency exchanges.

Regulation of Cryptocurrency Exchanges

Another global trend is the increased regulation of cryptocurrency exchanges. This trend can affect XRP in various ways. On the one hand, stricter regulations can lead to delistings, as was the case when several U.S. exchanges delisted XRP following the SEC lawsuit. On the other hand, well-regulated exchanges can attract more institutional investors, potentially increasing liquidity and stability for XRP.

Regulation of Cross-Border Payments

Regulatory trends in cross-border payments, a key use case for XRP, also significantly impact XRP. As more countries adopt regulatory frameworks that allow for and oversee blockchain-based cross-border payments, this could open up more opportunities for XRP to be used in this context. Ripple's On-Demand Liquidity service, which uses XRP as a bridge currency for cross-border transactions, stands to benefit from such trends.

Anti-Money Laundering (AML) and Know Your Customer (KYC) Regulations

Another significant regulatory trend is the increasing focus on Anti-Money Laundering (AML) and Know Your Customer (KYC) regulations. Cryptocurrencies have been associated with money laundering due to their pseudonymous nature, and regulators worldwide are working to mitigate these risks.

As a cryptocurrency that is often used by regulated financial institutions, XRP can potentially be impacted by these regulations. Compliance with AML and KYC regulations can make XRP more appealing to these institutions, as it reduces the risk of regulatory penalties.

Central Bank Digital Currencies (CBDCs)

The emergence of Central Bank Digital Currencies (CBDCs) is another trend to watch. The development of CBDCs indicates recognition of digital assets' potential by central banks worldwide, which could bode well for established cryptocurrencies like XRP. However, CBDCs could also present competition for certain use cases of XRP, such as cross-border transactions.

In conclusion, XRP's position within the global regulatory trends is complex and multifaceted. Each trend can present both opportunities and challenges for XRP. It's essential for anyone involved with XRP to stay informed about these trends and understand their potential impacts on XRP.

18.4 The Future of Cryptocurrency Regulation and Its Impact on XRP

The future of cryptocurrency regulation is subject to a multitude of factors and is likely to significantly impact the trajectory of XRP. In this section, we will examine some of the potential future regulatory scenarios and their implications for XRP.

Clarification of Legal Status

One of the most significant issues for XRP is the ongoing legal battle with the U.S. Securities and Exchange

Commission (SEC) over whether XRP should be classified as a security. The outcome of this case will have a profound impact on XRP's future, as a security designation could limit its use in the Ripple ecosystem and potentially result in penalties for Ripple.

If XRP is not deemed a security, it could boost investor confidence and open up more opportunities for XRP use within and beyond Ripple's payment system. In either scenario, the clarification of XRP's legal status would reduce uncertainty, which is generally positive for market stability.

Global Standardization of Cryptocurrency Regulation

There is a growing call for global standardization of cryptocurrency regulation. If achieved, this would likely boost the overall adoption of cryptocurrencies, including XRP. Standardized regulation could enable more seamless cross-border cryptocurrency transactions, a key use case for XRP.

However, the process of reaching global regulatory consensus is likely to be complex and time-consuming, given the varying perspectives of different jurisdictions on cryptocurrency regulation.

Increased Regulatory Scrutiny

As the cryptocurrency market continues to grow and mature, it is likely to attract increased regulatory scrutiny.

This could result in stricter regulations, particularly in areas such as anti-money laundering (AML) and consumer protection.

Increased regulatory scrutiny could be a double-edged sword for XRP. On the one hand, it could lead to more stringent compliance requirements, potentially increasing the operational costs for Ripple and other XRP users. On the other hand, if Ripple and XRP can successfully navigate this stricter regulatory environment, it could enhance XRP's credibility and attractiveness to institutional investors and regulated entities.

Regulation of Decentralized Finance (DeFi)

The rise of decentralized finance (DeFi) is another trend that could shape the future of cryptocurrency regulation. As of mid-2023, DeFi is still a largely unregulated space, but this is likely to change as it continues to grow and intersect with traditional finance.

If DeFi becomes heavily regulated, it could affect Ripple's exploration of DeFi use cases for XRP. However, it could also create opportunities for Ripple and XRP if they can provide compliant solutions in the DeFi space.

The future of cryptocurrency regulation holds both potential opportunities and challenges for XRP. As always, staying informed about regulatory developments and their potential impacts is crucial for anyone involved with XRP.

Chapter 19: The technology behind Ripple: how it powers XRP

19.1 Understanding Blockchain and Distributed Ledger Technology

The technology behind Ripple and its cryptocurrency, XRP, is based on principles of blockchain and distributed ledger technology (DLT). While these terms are often used interchangeably, they are distinct concepts, and understanding them is fundamental to understanding Ripple and XRP.

Blockchain Technology

Blockchain technology is a specific type of distributed ledger technology. The term "blockchain" comes from the structure of the technology, where data is grouped together into blocks, and each block is chained to the previous block through cryptographic hashes. This structure creates an immutable, transparent ledger of transactions that is resistant to tampering.

Each block contains a list of transactions, and once a block is added to the chain, the transactions within it are considered confirmed and permanent. The immutability of blockchain technology is one of its key features, providing a reliable, tamper-proof record of transactions.

Distributed Ledger Technology (DLT)

Distributed Ledger Technology (DLT) is a broader term that refers to technologies that distribute records or information among a network of participants. This distribution is what makes DLTs decentralized—instead of a single, central authority holding the master copy of the ledger, each participant in the network has a copy of the entire ledger.

DLTs use various consensus mechanisms to agree on the state of the ledger. In a blockchain, this is typically achieved through a process called mining, where participants (known as miners) solve complex mathematical problems to add new blocks to the chain. However, not all DLTs use this process. Ripple, for example, uses a consensus protocol that doesn't involve mining.

DLT and Blockchain in the Context of Ripple and XRP

Ripple's technology, which powers XRP, is a form of DLT known as the XRP Ledger (XRPL). It shares many features with blockchain technology, such as transparency, immutability, and decentralization. However, it differs in several key ways.

First, the XRPL does not group transactions into blocks. Instead, each transaction is validated individually. This allows for faster confirmation times compared to many blockchains.

Second, the XRPL uses a different consensus mechanism, known as the Ripple Protocol consensus algorithm, which doesn't require the energy-intensive mining process used in many blockchains. This consensus mechanism involves validators, which are nodes in the network that vote on the validity of transactions.

By understanding the principles of blockchain and distributed ledger technology, we can better appreciate the unique technological characteristics of Ripple and XRP, which will be further explored in the subsequent sections of this chapter.

19.2 The Ripple Protocol Consensus Algorithm Explained

The Ripple Protocol Consensus Algorithm (RPCA) is the consensus mechanism employed by the XRP Ledger (XRPL). Unlike many blockchain technologies that utilize proof-of-work (PoW) or proof-of-stake (PoS) mechanisms, the XRP Ledger utilizes this unique protocol that allows for faster, more efficient transaction validation. To fully grasp how the RPCA works, it's important to first understand the concept of consensus and its role in distributed ledger technologies.

Consensus in Distributed Ledger Technologies

In distributed ledger technologies, consensus mechanisms play a vital role in validating transactions and maintaining the integrity and security of the network. Consensus mechanisms ensure that all nodes or participants in the network agree on the validity of transactions and the current state of the ledger, thus preventing double spending and other forms of fraud.

How the Ripple Protocol Consensus Algorithm Works

The RPCA operates based on a group of validators, which are nodes that participate in the consensus process. These validators don't have to be trusted, and their selection is not centralized. Any node can be a validator, and each node chooses a Unique Node List (UNL), a list of validators that it individually decides to trust.

The RPCA follows several steps to reach consensus:

1. **Initialization:** At the beginning of each consensus round, every validator gathers transactions from the network, validating them against the current ledger's rules.
2. **Voting:** Each validator then proposes its set of valid transactions to the other validators on its UNL. Validators vote on the accuracy of all transactions, and transactions that receive more than a minimum percentage of 'yes' votes are passed onto the next round. This process is iterated several times to filter out potentially problematic transactions.

3. **Agreement:** After several rounds of voting, the remaining transactions require an 80% agreement from the validators. Any transaction that gets at least 80% votes is included in the next ledger.
4. **Validation and Ledger Creation:** Once consensus is reached, the new ledger is created, and each validator computes a new ledger hash, a unique identifier for the ledger. The validators then broadcast a validation message, along with the ledger hash, to the entire network. Once a node sees a supermajority of its trusted validators agreeing on a ledger hash, it accepts that ledger as validated.

Benefits of the Ripple Protocol Consensus Algorithm

The RPCA allows for faster transaction confirmation times compared to PoW or PoS mechanisms, as it doesn't require mining or staking. This makes the XRPL highly scalable and capable of settling transactions in 3-5 seconds.

The RPCA is also more energy-efficient than PoW, as it doesn't require massive computational power. This makes XRP more environmentally friendly compared to cryptocurrencies like Bitcoin.

The Ripple Protocol Consensus Algorithm is a cornerstone of the XRP Ledger's functionality. By offering speed, scalability, and energy efficiency, it supports the Ledger's goal of enabling fast, low-cost international transactions.

The Interledger Protocol (ILP) is an open protocol suite developed by Ripple for sending payments across different ledgers. Like routers on the Internet, connectors route packets of money across independent payment networks. The open architecture and minimal protocol enable interoperability for any value transfer system. ILP is not tied to any one company, blockchain, or currency, making it an important technology in the broader digital asset ecosystem.

Interledger Protocol Explained

The core principle of ILP is to provide a framework for different payment systems to interact seamlessly with each other. It does this by establishing a set of standards for how payment transactions should be sent across different ledgers.

ILP works by breaking down the payment transaction into small packets of money. These packets are then routed across different payment networks (which could be different blockchains or traditional banking systems) by connectors, which are the equivalent of routers in the ILP.

A critical aspect of ILP is that it provides for secure transactions across different networks, without the need for any party to trust any other party in the network. It does this by using cryptographic escrow and a system of balances and credits between connectors, ensuring that funds can't be lost or stolen during the transaction.

The Role of ILP in XRP and Ripple's Ecosystem

While ILP is ledger-agnostic and can work with any form of currency, it plays a significant role in Ripple's ecosystem. Ripple uses ILP to enable its payment and liquidity solutions, including RippleNet and On-Demand Liquidity (ODL).

RippleNet, Ripple's global payments network, uses ILP to enable frictionless transfer of money across countries. It allows banks and other financial institutions in the network to transact with each other, regardless of the underlying infrastructure of their payment systems.

Ripple's ODL service, which uses XRP as a bridge currency for cross-border transactions, also leverages ILP. When a financial institution wants to send money from one country to another using ODL, ILP is used to coordinate the transfer of XRP across the XRP Ledger and the transfer of fiat currencies across traditional payment systems.

Interledger Protocol and the Future of Payments

The Interledger Protocol represents a significant step forward in the vision of creating a fully interoperable global payment network. By providing a protocol for connecting different payment networks, ILP could play a crucial role in realizing the full potential of blockchain technology in revolutionizing how money is transferred around the world. As such, understanding ILP is key not only to understanding Ripple's technology stack and how XRP is used within it, but also to grasping the broader trends and possibilities in the world of digital payments.

19.4 Advanced Technological Features of the XRP Ledger

The XRP Ledger (XRPL) is a decentralized cryptographic ledger powered by a peer-to-peer network of nodes. It's the technology that underpins XRP, the digital asset for payments. Beyond its use of the Ripple Protocol Consensus Algorithm, the XRPL also boasts a number of advanced features that make it a highly efficient and versatile tool for financial transactions.

Scalability

The XRPL has been designed to easily handle a high throughput of transactions. It's capable of sustaining a throughput of 1,500 transactions per second, on par with traditional financial systems like Visa. This scalability makes the XRPL an effective ledger for global financial transactions.

Speed

Speed is one of the key selling points of the XRPL. Unlike Bitcoin and Ethereum, which can take minutes to hours to finalize transactions, the XRPL settles transactions in 3-5 seconds. This rapid settlement time is made possible by the consensus algorithm, which doesn't require mining.

Low Cost

Transaction fees on the XRPL are exceptionally low, typically amounting to a fraction of a cent. This makes XRP transactions cost-effective, particularly for cross-border money transfers that can otherwise incur high fees.

Decentralization

Despite misconceptions, the XRPL is decentralized. While Ripple contributes to its development, the ledger itself operates independently of any one entity. Validators on the network, which can be run by anyone, participate in the consensus process to validate and record transactions.

Security

The XRPL uses advanced cryptographic techniques to ensure the security and integrity of the ledger. The use of cryptographic signatures ensures that only the holder of the private key can authorize transactions from a given account.

Built-in Decentralized Exchange (DEX)

One unique feature of the XRPL is its built-in decentralized exchange. Users can trade any type of asset issued on the XRPL directly on the ledger. This includes not only XRP but also any other assets that users choose to issue, such as other cryptocurrencies or fiat currency tokens. The DEX also supports advanced trading features like order books and escrow for secure, conditional payments.

Interoperability

With the Interledger Protocol, the XRPL is designed for interoperability with other cryptocurrencies and payment networks. This means that payments can be sent across different networks, further enhancing the reach and utility of XRP.

The XRP Ledger offers advanced features that make it a robust, efficient, and versatile platform for global financial transactions. Its strengths lie in its speed, scalability, and low cost, while its built-in decentralized exchange and support for interoperability offer flexibility and reach. By understanding these features, one can better appreciate the potential of XRP and its role in the digital asset ecosystem.

Chapter 20: XRP and the emergence of crypto-based financial products

20.1 Introduction to Crypto-Based Financial Products

As cryptocurrencies have gained popularity and acceptance, a new generation of financial products based on these digital assets has emerged. These crypto-based financial products provide traditional financial services, such as lending, borrowing, and investing, but with the benefits of blockchain technology, including transparency, decentralization, and programmability. This section provides an introduction to crypto-based financial products, setting the stage for further discussions about XRP's role in this evolving landscape.

What Are Crypto-Based Financial Products?

Crypto-based financial products are financial services that use cryptocurrencies as the underlying asset. These products mirror traditional financial services but are built on blockchain technology. They range from simple services such as cryptocurrency wallets and exchanges to more complex offerings like decentralized finance (DeFi) applications, which include lending, borrowing, insurance, and derivatives trading platforms.

Types of Crypto-Based Financial Products

The following are some of the key types of crypto-based financial products:

Cryptocurrency Exchanges and Wallets: These are the most basic types of crypto-based financial products. Exchanges allow users to trade cryptocurrencies, while wallets provide storage for these digital assets.

Crypto Lending and Borrowing Platforms: These platforms enable users to lend their cryptocurrencies to earn interest or borrow cryptocurrencies by providing collateral. These services can be centralized, run by a specific company, or decentralized, run on a blockchain protocol.

Crypto Derivatives: These are financial contracts that derive their value from an underlying cryptocurrency. They can be used for hedging risk, speculating on price movements, or gaining access to assets without owning them outright.

Crypto Funds and ETFs: These are investment funds that hold a portfolio of cryptocurrencies. They provide a way for investors to gain exposure to a diversified set of cryptocurrencies without the need to manage individual assets.

Stablecoins: These are cryptocurrencies pegged to a stable asset, such as a fiat currency. They provide a way to transact in cryptocurrencies while avoiding the volatility typically associated with these assets.

Decentralized Exchanges (DEXs): These are platforms that allow for direct peer-to-peer trading of cryptocurrencies, without the need for an intermediary.

Yield Farming and Liquidity Mining Platforms: These are DeFi platforms that incentivize users to provide liquidity to a platform by rewarding them with a return, often in the platform's native token.

Insurance Protocols: These are platforms that provide coverage for various risks associated with cryptocurrency, such as smart contract failures or exchange hacks.

Benefits and Risks of Crypto-Based Financial Products

Crypto-based financial products offer several advantages over traditional financial products, including accessibility, transparency, programmability, and potential for high returns. However, they also come with their own set of risks, including high volatility, regulatory uncertainty, technical risks, and market manipulation.

It's crucial to understand these dynamics as we delve into the specific role of XRP in the landscape of crypto-based financial products. The following sections will explore how XRP is being used in lending and borrowing platforms, investment funds, insurance, and more, reflecting its multifaceted utility in the rapidly growing world of crypto finance.

Crypto lending and borrowing platforms have gained significant attention in recent years, providing a new avenue for cryptocurrency holders to earn interest on their holdings and access liquidity. Among the various cryptocurrencies used in these platforms, XRP has found its unique place due to its high-speed transactions and low fees.

Crypto Lending and Borrowing: An Overview

Crypto lending platforms enable users to lend their cryptocurrency assets to others in exchange for interest payments. On the other side, borrowers can obtain loans in cryptocurrency, often by providing some form of collateral, usually in another cryptocurrency. This system allows lenders to earn passive income on their cryptocurrency holdings while providing borrowers with a way to access funds without selling their assets.

These platforms operate either in a centralized or decentralized manner. Centralized platforms are managed by a single entity, while decentralized platforms (also known as DeFi or decentralized finance platforms) operate on a blockchain and use smart contracts to automate lending and borrowing processes.

Role of XRP in Crypto Lending and Borrowing

XRP, the native cryptocurrency of the Ripple network, has gained popularity on crypto lending platforms for several reasons:

Fast and Low-Cost Transactions: XRP transactions settle in just 3-5 seconds and incur very low fees. This makes XRP an attractive option for lending and borrowing platforms, where speed and cost-efficiency are valuable.

Liquidity: XRP is one of the most liquid cryptocurrencies, with a large market cap and wide adoption. This high liquidity makes it suitable as both a lending and borrowing asset.

Stability: While XRP, like all cryptocurrencies, experiences price volatility, it is often perceived as one of the more stable large-cap cryptocurrencies. This relative stability can be attractive to lenders and borrowers looking to manage their risk.

Many lending platforms have recognized these advantages and incorporated XRP into their offerings. For example, platforms like Nexo, Celsius, and Bitrue allow users to earn interest on their XRP deposits and use XRP as collateral for loans.

Considerations and Risks

While XRP and crypto lending platforms present exciting opportunities, they also come with risks. These include the volatility of XRP's price, the potential for platform failure or hacks, and the regulatory uncertainty surrounding crypto lending. It's crucial that users thoroughly understand these risks and the specific terms of their lending or borrowing agreement before participating in crypto lending with XRP or any other cryptocurrency.

XRP's role in crypto lending and borrowing highlights its utility beyond simple transfers of value. Through crypto lending platforms, XRP holders can generate passive income or access liquidity, contributing to the broader use and integration of XRP in the financial system.

20.3 XRP-based ETFs and Investment Funds

As the cryptocurrency sector has matured, we have seen the development of a variety of investment vehicles that allow for exposure to these digital assets. Among these are Exchange Traded Funds (ETFs) and investment funds that are based on or include XRP.

XRP-Based ETFs: An Overview

An Exchange Traded Fund (ETF) is a type of investment fund and exchange-traded product, i.e., they are traded on stock exchanges. ETFs are designed to track the price of a particular asset or group of assets. In the context of cryptocurrencies, a crypto ETF, such as an XRP-based ETF, would be designed to track the price of XRP.

The goal of an XRP-based ETF would be to provide investors with the opportunity to gain exposure to the performance of XRP without the need to directly purchase and securely store the cryptocurrency. This structure can potentially lower the barriers to entry for individuals or institutions interested in the cryptocurrency market but who may not have the technical knowledge or infrastructure to handle these digital assets directly.

XRP in Investment Funds

Beyond ETFs, there are also various types of investment funds that include XRP as part of their portfolio. These might be mutual funds, hedge funds, or private equity funds that have a focus on digital assets. In these cases, XRP is often one of several cryptocurrencies included in the fund's portfolio.

These funds provide a way for investors to gain diversified exposure to the cryptocurrency market. They are typically managed by professional fund managers who make decisions about when to buy and sell assets within the fund's portfolio. For investors who are not comfortable managing their own cryptocurrency investments, these funds can provide a more hands-off way to invest in XRP and other digital assets.

Regulatory Environment and Challenges

It's crucial to note that the regulatory environment for XRP-based ETFs and other investment funds is still developing.

As of my knowledge cut-off in September 2021, no XRP-based ETF had been approved by major financial regulators like the U.S. Securities and Exchange Commission (SEC). However, the situation may have changed since then.

There are also important regulatory considerations for investment funds that include XRP in their portfolio. For instance, in the U.S., these funds may be subject to the rules and regulations of the SEC, the Commodity Futures Trading Commission (CFTC), and potentially other regulatory bodies.

Conclusion

XRP-based ETFs and investment funds can provide investors with exposure to the price movements of XRP without the need to directly purchase and store the cryptocurrency. However, like all investment vehicles, they come with risks, and investors should carefully consider these risks before investing. The development of these financial products is a testament to the growing recognition and acceptance of XRP and other digital assets in the mainstream financial world.

20.4 XRP in Insurance and Risk Management

In the context of the evolving digital economy, the insurance industry is in a unique position to leverage the power of cryptocurrencies like XRP, both for financial transactions and risk management.

Crypto Insurance: An Overview

Crypto insurance refers to coverage for risks associated with cryptocurrencies and blockchain technology. The increased adoption of digital assets has led to an increased demand for insurance coverage for risks such as theft, hacking, and operational errors. This is an emerging field, with several insurance companies beginning to offer policies that cover cryptocurrency-related risks.

Role of XRP in Insurance

XRP, with its quick settlement times and low transaction costs, can play a significant role in the insurance sector in several ways:

Claims Settlement: XRP could be used to settle insurance claims quickly. The speed of XRP transactions could enable insurers to pay out claims in near real-time, improving customer experience.

Premium Payments: Insurers could accept premium payments in XRP. This could be particularly useful for international customers, allowing them to avoid currency conversion fees and delays associated with traditional banking systems.

Reinsurance: XRP could be used in the reinsurance market, where insurance companies insure their risks with other insurers. Transactions in this market are often complex and cross-border, making the speed and low cost of XRP transactions highly beneficial.

XRP and Risk Management

Cryptocurrencies like XRP can also play a role in risk management within the insurance industry. For instance, insurance companies could use XRP as a form of diversification, holding a portion of their assets in XRP or other cryptocurrencies to spread their risk.

Additionally, blockchain technology, which underpins XRP, can also be used for risk management. The transparency and immutability of blockchain can help insurers better track and manage risks, potentially reducing instances of fraud and improving efficiency.

Considerations and Challenges

While the use of XRP in insurance and risk management presents potential benefits, there are also challenges and risks to consider. These include the price volatility of XRP, regulatory uncertainty around the use of cryptocurrencies in the insurance industry, and the technical challenges of integrating digital assets into existing systems and processes.

While still in the early stages, the use of XRP in the insurance industry holds promising potential for improving efficiency, reducing costs, and enhancing risk management practices. As the insurance industry continues to evolve and adapt to the digital age, it's likely that we'll see increased experimentation with and adoption of digital assets like XRP.

20.5 The Future of XRP in Financial Products and Services

The integration of XRP into the realm of financial products and services is part of a broader trend of cryptocurrency adoption across diverse sectors of the economy. The inherent features of XRP, such as fast transaction times, low fees, and scalability, make it an attractive digital asset for the future of finance. Here are some ways XRP might shape the future of financial products and services:

Decentralized Finance (DeFi):

Decentralized finance (DeFi) is a term for financial services that operate without traditional intermediaries such as banks, brokerages, or insurance companies. Instead, DeFi applications run on blockchain networks and utilize smart contracts. While the majority of DeFi is currently built on the Ethereum network, the potential for XRP in this space is considerable. Ripple has even launched Flare, a network that brings Ethereum's smart contract functionality to the

XRP ecosystem, signifying a commitment to engage with DeFi.

Cross-border Payments and Remittances:

One area where XRP has already made significant inroads is in the realm of cross-border payments and remittances. XRP's speed and low transaction costs make it ideally suited for international transactions. Ripple's payment technology, RippleNet, uses XRP for liquidity and enables financial institutions to transfer money globally in seconds. In the future, more banks and payment services could adopt this technology, leading to increased use of XRP.

Central Bank Digital Currencies (CBDCs):

As nations explore the development of their own digital currencies, XRP could play a key role as a bridge currency, enabling quick and efficient conversion between different CBDCs. This could simplify and expedite international transactions involving different national digital currencies.

Expansion of XRP-Based Financial Products:

As regulatory clarity improves and the crypto market continues to mature, we can expect to see a proliferation of XRP-based financial products, such as XRP ETFs, lending platforms, and insurance products. These products will offer individuals and institutions more ways to gain exposure to XRP and could drive additional liquidity and demand for the asset.

Tokenization and Smart Contracts:

With developments like the Flare Network, XRP could be increasingly used in tokenization and smart contracts. Tokenization could bring real-world assets onto the blockchain, while smart contracts could automate the execution of agreements, both potentially creating new use cases for XRP.

Integration into Existing Financial Infrastructure:

XRP and Ripple's associated technologies might be further integrated into existing financial infrastructure, not just for cross-border payments, but also for securities settlement, trade finance, and other applications.

Challenges Ahead:

While the potential is vast, challenges remain. Regulatory uncertainty is a significant hurdle, especially given the ongoing legal issues between Ripple Labs and the SEC (as of my last update in September 2021). Moreover, the volatility of XRP and other cryptocurrencies can present risks for some types of financial services.

The future of XRP in financial products and services is promising, but not without its challenges. The continued development and adoption of XRP will likely depend on a variety of factors, including technological innovation, regulatory developments, and broader market trends. As these factors evolve, so too will the role of XRP in the world of finance.

Message from the Author:

Dear Reader,

As we come to the end of this journey through the world of XRP, I hope that you have gained a deeper understanding of this cryptocurrency, its use cases, and the potential it holds for transforming the financial landscape. It is important to remember that I am not a financial advisor, and this book should not be taken as financial advice. The information provided is meant to educate and inform, helping you make your own informed decisions regarding XRP and its place in your investment portfolio or business.

Throughout this book, we have explored the legitimacy of XRP and its potential impact on the global economy. From its role in cross-border payments and remittances to its potential as a reserve currency, the diverse applications of XRP make it an important player in the ever-evolving world of digital assets. By understanding the various aspects of XRP and the Ripple ecosystem, you are now better equipped to appreciate its significance and potential for growth.

As the landscape of cryptocurrencies and blockchain technology continues to change, it is crucial to stay informed and adapt to new developments. I encourage you to continue exploring the world of XRP and other digital assets, as they hold the key to unlocking new opportunities in the digital age. Remember, the future is not set in stone, and it is up to us to shape it.

Thank you for joining me on this journey, and I wish you all the best in your endeavors in the world of XRP and beyond.

Warm regards,

Aidan Carmody

Side Note: Ripple and the SEC's Legal Battle

As you read through this book, it is important to note that Ripple, the company behind XRP, is currently engaged in a legal battle with the United States Securities and Exchange Commission (SEC). The SEC filed a lawsuit against Ripple in December 2020, alleging that the company's sale of XRP constituted an unregistered securities offering. Ripple has vehemently denied these allegations, asserting that XRP is a digital currency, not a security.

The outcome of this case will have significant implications for XRP and its future classification, as well as its position within the broader cryptocurrency landscape. The resolution of this legal battle may ultimately determine the regulatory treatment of XRP and could influence how other cryptocurrencies are classified and regulated in the future.

While the case has been ongoing for some time, it is expected to come to a conclusion soon, either through a settlement, a court decision, or even by escalating to the Supreme Court. It is essential to keep an eye on the developments of this case, as it may have a profound impact on the XRP ecosystem and the cryptocurrency industry as a whole.

Appendix A: Notable XRP and Ripple Partnerships

Over the years, Ripple has formed numerous partnerships with various companies and financial institutions worldwide. These partnerships have played a significant role in the growth and adoption of XRP, as well as the broader Ripple ecosystem. Some of the most notable partnerships include:

American Express: This global financial services company partnered with Ripple to enable instant blockchain-based payments, enhancing its cross-border payment services and reducing transaction times.

Standard Chartered: This multinational banking and financial services company has invested in Ripple and leverages its technology to facilitate faster, more transparent, and cost-effective cross-border transactions.

Santander: One of the world's largest banks, Santander, has integrated Ripple's technology into its One Pay FX mobile app, which allows customers in various countries to make fast and low-cost international money transfers.

SBI Holdings: This Japanese financial services company has been a long-time partner and investor in Ripple. SBI Holdings has also launched SBI Ripple Asia, a joint venture focused on promoting the adoption of Ripple's solutions in the Asian market.

MoneyGram: Before ending their partnership in 2021, MoneyGram utilized Ripple's xRapid (now known as ODL) solution for two years to facilitate real-time, low-cost cross-border payments using XRP as a bridge currency.

National Bank of Abu Dhabi (NBAD): The largest bank in the United Arab Emirates, NBAD, has integrated Ripple's technology to enhance its remittance services by providing faster, more secure, and more efficient cross-border transactions for its customers.

Bank of America: One of the largest banks in the United States, Bank of America, has been working with Ripple to explore the potential benefits of blockchain technology for streamlining cross-border payments.

PNC Bank: This major US-based bank has joined RippleNet to enable faster and more efficient cross-border transactions for its customers. By leveraging Ripple's technology, PNC Bank aims to improve the transparency and speed of international payments.

Banco Santander Brasil: The Brazilian subsidiary of Banco Santander has partnered with Ripple to streamline its cross-border payment services, enabling faster and more efficient transactions between Brazil and other countries.

BBVA: This multinational Spanish banking group has been exploring Ripple's technology for cross-border payments, aiming to reduce costs and improve transaction speed for its customers.

Bittrex, Bitso, and Coins.ph: These cryptocurrency exchanges partnered with Ripple to enable xRapid (ODL) transactions. By acting as liquidity providers, these exchanges facilitated near-instant cross-border payments using XRP as a bridge currency.

Azimo: This digital money transfer service leverages Ripple's ODL solution to offer fast and low-cost remittances to customers in various countries, particularly in emerging markets.

Nium (formerly InstaReM): This global fintech platform has partnered with Ripple to enhance its cross-border payment services, leveraging RippleNet to provide faster, more secure, and cost-effective transactions for its customers.

These partnerships represent only a fraction of the numerous collaborations Ripple has forged in its mission to revolutionize the global financial system. As the Ripple ecosystem continues to expand, more companies and financial institutions are expected to adopt XRP and Ripple's technology, further driving the growth and adoption of XRP.

B: Frequently Asked Questions (FAQs) About XRP and Ripple

What is XRP? XRP is a digital asset and cryptocurrency that powers the XRP Ledger, an open-source blockchain that facilitates fast and low-cost cross-border transactions.

What is Ripple? Ripple is a technology company that develops and maintains the RippleNet payment network and the XRP Ledger, aiming to enable instant and efficient global transactions.

How is XRP different from Ripple? XRP is the native cryptocurrency of the XRP Ledger, while Ripple is the company that created the ledger and the payment network, RippleNet.

How does XRP differ from Bitcoin and Ethereum? XRP is designed for faster transaction speeds, lower fees, and better scalability compared to Bitcoin and Ethereum. It uses a consensus protocol instead of proof-of-work or proof-of-stake.

Can I mine XRP like Bitcoin? No, XRP cannot be mined as all XRP tokens were pre-mined before the launch of the XRP Ledger.

How do I buy XRP? You can buy XRP from various cryptocurrency exchanges using fiat currencies or other cryptocurrencies.

How do I store my XRP? You can store XRP in a compatible wallet, such as a hardware wallet, software wallet, or paper wallet.

Is XRP safe and secure? Yes, XRP is considered safe and secure due to its consensus protocol and decentralized network of validators.

How does the XRP Ledger achieve consensus? The XRP Ledger uses the Ripple Protocol Consensus Algorithm (RPCA), which relies on validators to agree on the validity of transactions.

What is RippleNet? RippleNet is a global payment network developed by Ripple that connects banks, payment providers, and other financial institutions for faster and more efficient cross-border transactions.

How does XRP reduce transaction costs? XRP serves as a bridge currency, enabling the conversion between different fiat currencies, reducing the need for intermediary banks, and lowering transaction costs.

Is XRP considered a security, currency, or commodity? XRP's classification is still a matter of debate and may vary by jurisdiction. In some countries, it is treated as a currency, while in others, it is considered a commodity or security.

What is the maximum supply of XRP? The maximum supply of XRP is 100 billion tokens, with about 46 billion in circulation as of September 2021.

What is the role of validators in the XRP Ledger? Validators participate in the consensus process, verifying transactions, and maintaining the integrity of the XRP Ledger.

What are the use cases for XRP? XRP's primary use cases include cross-border payments, remittances, liquidity provisioning, micropayments, and decentralized finance (DeFi).

Can I earn interest on my XRP holdings? Some platforms and services allow users to earn interest on their XRP holdings through lending or staking.

Is XRP environmentally friendly? Yes, XRP is considered environmentally friendly due to its low energy consumption compared to proof-of-work cryptocurrencies like Bitcoin.

What is the Internet of Value (IoV)? The Internet of Value is a vision for seamless, instant, and low-cost transfer of value, similar to how information is transferred over the internet.

How does XRP fit into the Internet of Value? XRP aims to facilitate the Internet of Value by enabling fast, low-cost, and secure global transactions.

What are Central Bank Digital Currencies (CBDCs), and how do they relate to XRP? CBDCs are digital currencies issued by central banks that can be used for payments and settlements. XRP can facilitate the exchange between CBDCs and other digital assets.

What is the Flare Network, and how does it relate to XRP? The Flare Network is a separate blockchain designed to bring smart contract functionality to various cryptocurrencies, including XRP. By integrating with the XRP Ledger, it enables developers to create and deploy smart contracts for XRP-based use cases, expanding the utility and applications of XRP in the decentralized finance (DeFi) space.

Can XRP be used for micropayments and web monetization? Yes, XRP can be used for micropayments and web monetization due to its fast transaction speeds and low fees.

What is Coil, and how does it use XRP? Coil is a web monetization platform that uses XRP to enable micropayments for content creators and users.

What is xCurrent, xRapid, and xVia? xCurrent, xRapid, and xVia are the three main components of RippleNet. xCurrent facilitates real-time messaging and settlement, xRapid uses XRP for liquidity provisioning, and xVia allows users to send payments through a standardized interface.

Can XRP be used in decentralized finance (DeFi)? Yes, XRP can be used in decentralized finance applications, such as lending, borrowing, and trading on decentralized exchanges.

Is XRP centralized or decentralized? XRP is considered decentralized, as it operates on a distributed network of validators that maintain the XRP Ledger.

What is the ongoing SEC vs. Ripple lawsuit about? The SEC vs. Ripple lawsuit centers around the classification of XRP as a security, with the SEC alleging that Ripple conducted an unregistered securities offering.

What are the potential outcomes of the SEC vs. Ripple lawsuit? The outcomes could include a settlement, a ruling that XRP is a security, or a ruling that XRP is not a security. The case could also potentially reach the Supreme Court. What is the XRPL Labs? XRPL Labs is a development company focused on creating tools, applications, and services for the XRP Ledger ecosystem.

What are some popular XRP wallets? Some popular XRP wallets include Ledger Nano, Trezor, Exodus, and Toast Wallet.

What are the tax implications of holding and trading XRP? Tax implications for XRP holders and traders may vary by jurisdiction, but generally, profits from trading or selling XRP are subject to capital gains tax.

How do I report XRP transactions for tax purposes? You can use specialized cryptocurrency tax software or consult with a tax professional to accurately report your XRP transactions.

Can I send XRP to a non-XRP address? No, sending XRP to a non-XRP address will result in the loss of your XRP. Always double-check the destination address before initiating a transaction.

What is the minimum reserve requirement on the XRP Ledger? The minimum reserve requirement on the XRP Ledger is 20 XRP, which is held to maintain an active account.

How can I recover my XRP if I lose my wallet or private keys? Unfortunately, if you lose your wallet or private keys, it is nearly impossible to recover your XRP. It is crucial to securely store your private keys and wallet backups.

Can I stake XRP like other cryptocurrencies? XRP does not have a native staking mechanism, but some platforms allow users to earn interest on their XRP through lending or other methods.

How can I track the price of XRP? You can track the price of XRP on various cryptocurrency market tracking websites or apps, such as CoinMarketCap, CoinGecko, or Delta.

Are there any XRP-based stablecoins? Yes, there are stablecoins built on the XRP Ledger, such as USDX (USD-pegged) and EURX (EUR-pegged).

Can I use XRP for remittances? Yes, XRP is designed to facilitate fast and low-cost cross-border transactions, making it an ideal option for remittances.

What are some businesses that accept XRP as payment? Several businesses accept XRP

Can I use XRP for online shopping? Yes, some online merchants and payment gateways accept XRP as a payment method for goods and services.

What are some notable partnerships involving XRP and Ripple? Notable partnerships include American Express, Santander, Standard Chartered, SBI Holdings, and MoneyGram.

What is the XRP Community? The XRP Community is a group of individuals, developers, and businesses that support, promote, and contribute to the growth and development of the XRP ecosystem.

What is the role of XRP in Ripple's On-Demand Liquidity (ODL) service? XRP serves as a bridge currency in ODL, enabling instant and cost-effective cross-border transactions by providing liquidity on demand.

How does XRP contribute to financial inclusion? XRP can help improve financial inclusion by providing faster, cheaper, and more accessible cross-border payments and remittance services to the unbanked and underbanked populations.

What is the XRP Tip Bot? The XRP Tip Bot is a service that enables users to send and receive XRP tips on social media platforms like Twitter, Reddit, and Discord.

Can XRP be used for smart contracts? While the XRP Ledger does not natively support smart contracts, the Flare Network, a separate blockchain, aims to bring smart contract functionality to XRP.

How do I choose the right XRP wallet? Consider factors such as security, user experience, backup and recovery options, and device compatibility when choosing an XRP wallet.

Are there any XRP-based decentralized exchanges? Yes, some decentralized exchanges, like Sologenic DEX, support XRP-based trading pairs and allow users to trade XRP against other digital assets.

How do I avoid scams and phishing attacks involving XRP? Always double-check addresses, use secure wallets and exchanges, enable two-factor authentication, and be cautious when participating in XRP giveaways or promotions.

Ripple v. SEC: A Landmark Case in Cryptocurrency Regulation

The Ripple v. SEC case is a pivotal lawsuit in the United States Southern District Court of New York that could shape the future of cryptocurrency regulations. The case revolves around whether cryptocurrencies, specifically Ripple's XRP token, should be classified as a security or a commodity.

In 2020, the U.S. Securities and Exchange Commission (SEC) accused Ripple, the blockchain developer and creator of the XRP cryptocurrency token, of raising over $1 billion in 2013 through an unregistered security offering. Ripple, however, argues that XRP should not be treated as a security, citing previous comments from an SEC director to support its case.

The outcome of this case could have far-reaching implications for the cryptocurrency industry. An SEC victory could potentially make the SEC the primary regulator for cryptocurrencies, leading to tighter regulations and potentially more legal actions against other crypto projects.

Ripple Labs, founded in 2012, launched the XRP token as a solution for fast, cross-border remittances. However, the

SEC's lawsuit in December 2020 led to a suspension of XRP trading on major crypto exchanges, negatively impacting the token's market sentiment.

The SEC's lawsuit also charges Ripple's executives, Brad Garlinghouse and Christian Larsen, with selling unregulated securities valued at over $1.3 billion to the public. The case hinges on the definition of a coin sale, with the SEC arguing that it constitutes a security and must be registered, while Ripple contends that a crypto coin is not a security.

The case continues, with Ripple maintaining that there are no grounds for the action. The Chamber of Digital Commerce has also filed a 'friend of the court' brief on Ripple's behalf, emphasizing the far-reaching consequences of the court's decision.

This case represents a significant moment in the evolution of cryptocurrency regulation, with potential implications for the broader crypto market and the future of blockchain technology.

The Genesis of the Case

The Role of Ripple and XRP in the Cryptocurrency Market

Ripple, a centralized fintech company, has played a significant role in the cryptocurrency market through its development of the XRP payment system. Ripple's XRP is an independent digital asset that consistently lists among the top cryptocurrencies in the market. Ripple's primary aim was to provide secure payment options to members of an online community via a global network, a concept that reportedly predates Bitcoin by four to five years.

Ripple's XRP is quicker and cheaper at fractions of a penny and about three seconds faster per transaction compared to other digital assets. This efficiency has made XRP a popular choice for fast, cross-border remittances, positioning Ripple as a key player in the global financial services industry.

The SEC's Initial Allegations Against Ripple

In December 2020, the U.S. Securities and Exchange Commission (SEC) filed an action against Ripple Labs Inc. and two of its executives, Christian Larsen, the company's co-founder, executive chairman of its board and former CEO, and Bradley Garlinghouse, the company's current CEO. The SEC alleged that they raised over $1.3 billion through an unregistered, ongoing digital asset securities offering.

The SEC's complaint stated that Ripple raised funds beginning in 2013 through the sale of digital assets known as XRP in an unregistered securities offering to investors in the U.S. and worldwide. Ripple also allegedly distributed billions of XRP in exchange for non-cash consideration, such as labor and market-making services.

In addition to structuring and promoting the XRP sales used to finance the company's business, Larsen and Garlinghouse also effected personal unregistered sales of XRP totaling approximately $600 million. The SEC alleged that the defendants failed to register their offers and sales of XRP or satisfy any exemption from registration, in violation of the registration provisions of the federal securities laws.

The SEC's action against Ripple marked a significant turning point in the regulation of cryptocurrencies, setting the stage for a legal battle that could have far-reaching implications for the cryptocurrency market.

The Legal Battle Begins

Ripple's Response to the SEC's Allegations

Ripple's response to the SEC's allegations has been robust and confident. Ripple CEO Brad Garlinghouse has expressed that the company's fight against the SEC's lawsuit has gone "exceedingly well," much better than he could have hoped when it began about 15 months ago. Ripple has disputed the SEC's findings, arguing that XRP should be treated as a virtual currency rather than an investment contract like a stock. Ripple believes that the lawsuit is not just important for Ripple, but for the entire crypto industry in the United States.

Key Legal Arguments and Counterarguments

A key point of contention in the legal battle has been the SEC's request to withhold certain documents. Ripple's lawyers have asked the court to reject this request, alleging that the SEC deliberately misread an order rejecting that request. The SEC had stated that the court should bar Ripple from seeking "irrelevant, privileged SEC staff materials" that the court had already ruled are not discoverable. However, Ripple's lawyers argue that the court had already rejected the arguments the SEC posed and that the SEC did not seek a reconsideration within the allowed fourteen-day period.

In another development, the SEC made a request that the court deny a motion from Ripple Labs that attempted to stop the SEC from contacting and acquiring documents from Ripple's foreign regulators. The SEC could potentially use these documents against Ripple in their lawsuit. This ongoing legal battle continues to unfold, with each side presenting their arguments and counterarguments in court.

The Impact on XRP and the Cryptocurrency Market

Market Reactions to the Case

The ongoing legal battle between Ripple and the SEC has had a significant impact on the cryptocurrency market, particularly on the performance of XRP. The market has been closely monitoring the developments in the case, and these developments have been reflected in the price of XRP. For instance, XRP rallied as much as 20% on a single day when Ripple made headway in its court case with the SEC. This shows that the market sentiment towards XRP is highly influenced by the progress of the lawsuit.

The Effect on XRP's Price and Trading

The lawsuit has also had a direct impact on the price and trading of XRP. The value of XRP has been fluctuating in response to the developments in the case. For example, when the judge in the case ordered the unsealing of some documents relating to the case, XRP's price shot up from $0.60 to $0.90 at one point. However, it's worth noting that the price of XRP can also be influenced by other factors in the cryptocurrency market.

In another instance, the price of LBC (a token related to a similar case between the SEC and LBRY) soared after a court decision, leading some to speculate that XRP could follow a similar trajectory if Ripple were to win the case. However, it's important to note that the outcome of the lawsuit is still uncertain, and its ultimate impact on XRP's price and trading will depend on the final ruling.

As the lawsuit continues, the price and trading of XRP will likely continue to be influenced by the developments in the case. The cryptocurrency community is closely watching the case, as its outcome could have far-reaching implications for the regulation of cryptocurrencies and the future of the cryptocurrency market.

The Turning Point
Significant Developments in the Case

The Ripple v. SEC case has seen several significant developments that have shaped the course of the legal battle. One of the key turning points was a discovery decision involving the SEC's deliberative process privilege. The SEC had argued that certain documents, including notes from meetings between the SEC and third parties, were protected by this privilege. However, the court rejected this interpretation, stating that fact gathering from third parties is not an inherently privileged activity. This ruling potentially opens the door to discovery of purely factual staff notes in other proceedings, marking a significant development in the case.

Another significant development was the court's decision on the SEC's request to withhold certain documents. Ripple's lawyers had asked the court to reject this request, alleging that the SEC deliberately misread an order rejecting that request. The court sided with Ripple on this matter, stating that the SEC had not demonstrated that the documents in question were prepared to help the SEC formulate its position.

The Release of Key Documents

The release of key documents has played a crucial role in the unfolding of the Ripple v. SEC case. These documents, which include notes from meetings and other communications, have provided valuable insights into the SEC's stance and strategy in the lawsuit. The court's decision to allow the discovery of these documents has been seen as a victory for Ripple, potentially strengthening its position in the legal battle.

As the case continues to unfold, these developments and the release of key documents will likely continue to shape the course of the legal battle, potentially influencing the final outcome of the case.

The Final Bids for a Quick Win

Ripple and the SEC's Final Arguments

As the Ripple v. SEC case nears its conclusion, both sides have made their final bids for a quick win. Ripple Labs Inc. and the SEC have accused each other of stretching the law in their arguments. Both sides have urged U.S. District Judge Analisa Torres to rule in their favor without sending the case to trial. The final round of briefs seeking summary judgment brings the case closer to a ruling that could further define what digital assets are considered securities in the U.S.

Ripple argued that the SEC was seeking a ruling that XRP was an investment contract but without any contract, without any investor rights, and without any issuer obligations. Ripple stated that the SEC is asking the court to rewrite the statutes that define its authority. On the other hand, the SEC argued that Ripple is relying on a made-up test that ignores U.S. securities law.

The Anticipation of a Ruling

The anticipation of a ruling in the Ripple v. SEC case is high. Ripple Labs Inc. has stated that a recent U.S. Supreme Court decision supports one of its key defenses in the case. The Supreme Court decision in question limited the government's ability to levy penalties on U.S. taxpayers who fail to report foreign bank accounts.

Ripple asked Judge Torres to consider this decision when she rules in the SEC's case.

The outcome of this case could have far-reaching implications for the cryptocurrency industry. The ruling could further define what digital assets are considered securities in the U.S., potentially influencing the regulatory landscape for cryptocurrencies. As such, the anticipation of a ruling in the Ripple v. SEC case is high, with the cryptocurrency industry closely watching the developments in the case.

The Aftermath and Implications

The Outcome of the Case and Its Implications

The outcome of the SEC vs. Ripple lawsuit will have far-reaching consequences for the cryptocurrency industry. If the SEC wins, it could establish itself as the primary regulator for cryptocurrencies in the U.S. This would potentially impose burdensome registration and reporting requirements on crypto firms, and may have legal consequences for entities that have issued tokens or helped people trade them without SEC approval.

The SEC's argument is that Ripple's ICO, and by extension other ICOs, is the sale of a security that must be registered. An SEC victory in court would effectively make the SEC the main crypto regulator. This could open the floodgates for similar actions against other crypto projects, likely leading to tighter regulation of the industry.

On the other hand, Ripple is arguing that its sale of XRP does not qualify as an investment contract because no contracts were signed when the transactions took place. Ripple also argues that XRP does not satisfy the prongs of the Howey Test, which is used to determine whether a transaction qualifies as an investment contract.

The Future of XRP and Ripple

The future of XRP and Ripple is uncertain and largely depends on the outcome of the case. If Ripple loses, it could face a hefty fine and there could also be further action against key executives, which could impact the development of the project. However, if Ripple wins, it could set a precedent for other cryptocurrencies facing similar legal challenges.

In the more immediate term, the case has already had a significant impact on XRP's price and trading. After the SEC filed the suit, crypto exchanges such as Coinbase suspended trading in XRP, which added to the negative sentiment surrounding the coin. The final ruling could also influence the future classification of cryptocurrencies and the clarity of regulations surrounding digital assets.

Regardless of the outcome, the case has already had a significant impact on the cryptocurrency industry and has brought attention to the need for clear, concise regulation. The case has also sparked discussions about the role of regulatory bodies in the crypto industry and the need for a unified approach to crypto regulation.

Made in the USA
Coppell, TX
21 February 2024

29259452R00134